THIS BOOK BELONGS TO

THE BOOK OF
HEROES
TALES OF HISTORY'S MOST DARING DUDES

CRISPIN BOYER

NATIONAL GEOGRAPHIC
WASHINGTON, D.C.

CONTENTS

CHAPTER SIX

ACTION HEROES

CHAPTER SEVEN

INSPIRING MINDS

CHAPTER EIGHT

OUTSTANDING ANIMALS

INTRODUCTION

NEED A HERO?

KNIGHTS IN SHINING ARMOR, LAWMEN IN WHITE HATS, SUPERHEROES IN COOL COSTUMES—the good guys are easy to spot in blockbusters, books, and the panels of graphic novels. But real-life heroes don't always dress the part or save the day with truck-chucking strength. *The Book of Heroes* is dedicated to daring dudes of every type: fictional and flesh-and-blood, famous and unsung, bold in battle or brave in the pursuit of peace, fearless on the playing field or dauntless in the lab.

BUT WHAT MAKES A HERO A HERO? Although the word has many meanings, heroes all tend to share these seven stupendous qualities ...

1. HEROES ARE COURAGEOUS: They overcome fear to risk their careers, reputations, or lives to help others.

2. HEROES DO THE RIGHT THING: They have a strong sense of wrong and right.

3. HEROES HAVE COMPASSION: They care about the well-being of others.

4. HEROES ARE COMPETENT: Smart and skilled, they have brains as well as guts.

5. HEROES ARE INSPIRING: They are leaders who bring out the best in others.

6. HEROES NEVER QUIT: They keep going no matter how badly they stumble and are determined to succeed.

7. HEROES LEAP TO ACTION: They offer help when others do nothing and even when no one is watching.

THINK YOU MIGHT HAVE THE RIGHT STUFF?

Dr. Philip Zimbardo, a psychologist who studies the causes of courageous and cowardly behavior, believes all kids are heroes waiting to happen. He encourages heroes-in-training to be aware of the feelings of others and to avoid inaction—the so-called bystander effect—when it's time to do the right thing. And heroic deeds aren't just one-time bursts of bravery, such as diving into raging seas to save a drowning man or pulling passengers from a flaming car. Heroism can involve a long quest to stand up for the downtrodden, discover a cure, invent a lifesaving gadget, or champion a just cause even if it's unpopular.

EXPLORE THE HALL OF HEROES AND SEE FOR YOURSELF.

From ancient mythology to modern times, from saving lives to fighting for your rights, the inspiring men inside might unlock your inner hero. Whether you wear a cool costume is up to you.

AS YOU READ THE BOOK OF HEROES, WATCH FOR THESE FEARLESS FEATURES ...

GUTSY GALS

Not all the good guys in *The Book of Heroes* are guys. Heroines shine bright in these snippets dedicated to wondrous women.

Heroism isn't always planned. Jump into the extraordinary situations that drove people to make daring decisions in a hurry.

MOMENT OF BRAVERY

CHAPTER ONE

LEADING MEN

Not every leader is a hero, and not every hero is a leader. Both possess a specific set of qualities—charm, courage, quick thinking, humility—that rarely combine in a single individual. But when they do, you get some of history's most famous heroes. From Honest Abe to Alexander the Great, from Bill Gates to Sitting Bull, get ready to meet the men (and women) who led and sometimes bled, who inspire even after they've retired or passed into history.

U.S. president Barack Obama waves to onlookers on the parade route of his 2013 inauguration.

ABRAHAM LINCOLN

HE MENDED A BROKEN NATION

A braham Lincoln was elected the 16th president of the United States in November 1860. When he took office five months later, the states were no longer united. Conflict had been building for years between the northern and southern states over the southern institution of slavery—an institution that Lincoln opposed. His election brought the issue to a boiling point. Eleven southern states seceded (or separated) from the Union and formed a new nation: the Confederate States of America. Lincoln was now president of a nation divided in two. He was determined to put it back together.

FROM COUNTRY BOY TO CONGRESSMAN

One of America's greatest leaders was born in a one-room log cabin in Kentucky, U.S.A. School wasn't an option for young Lincoln, who was too busy helping his struggling family farm the land and hunt for supper. Yet he was eager to learn and sought an education wherever he could, often teaching himself. He walked for miles to borrow books from neighbors. When his family moved to Illinois in 1830, the 22-year-old Lincoln struck out to make a living. He cut wood, worked as a postmaster, and ran a general store. He found he had a talent for telling stories and making friends. He was an everyday guy with a natural charm. People liked the lanky shop owner.

> "I DO THE VERY BEST I KNOW HOW—THE VERY BEST I CAN; AND I MEAN TO KEEP ON DOING SO UNTIL THE END."
> —ABRAHAM LINCOLN

FEARLESS FACTS

➔ **BORN:** February 12, 1809, Hodgenville, Kentucky, U.S.A. ➔ **DIED:** April 15, 1865, Washington, D.C.
➔ **OCCUPATION:** President of the United States, lawyer ➔ **BOLDEST MOMENT:** Freeing the slaves during the American Civil War

In 1834, Lincoln began dabbling in politics and was elected to the Illinois state legislature. He studied law and began practicing as a lawyer in 1837. He served a single term in the U.S. House of Representatives in 1847 before resuming his career as a lawyer.

A HOUSE DIVIDED

Meanwhile, the nation was becoming increasingly split over slavery, which the southern states relied on for their economy. Lincoln had come to believe it was an evil that was destroying the country. "A house divided against itself cannot stand," he once said.

In 1857, the U.S. Supreme Court decided that black people were not citizens with the same rights as white people. Lincoln blasted the decision. He ran for president in 1860 and won. Although Lincoln insisted he wouldn't end the institution of slavery in the southern states, he was determined not to let it spread to the border states or the North. People in the South despised Lincoln for his antislavery views. They saw his election as a threat to their way of life, and southern states soon began seceding from the Union. On April 12, 1861, the Civil War between the North and the South began.

DARK DAYS

Unlike Jefferson Davis, the president of the Confederate States of America, Lincoln had little military experience. But as he demonstrated in his younger days, he was a quick learner and his own best teacher. He threw himself into the study of strategy. He stretched the powers of the presidency to call up soldiers for the Union Army to put down the Confederacy.

The first year and a half of the Civil War went badly for the North. Lincoln faced opposition from his own advisers and generals. He had hoped to reunify the country quickly, even if that meant allowing slavery to continue in the South. The war took its toll on the president. In the span of a few years, he looked like he'd aged decades.

As the battles wore on, Lincoln's goals for victory and views on slavery evolved. No longer content with just preserving the Union, he also wanted to end slavery. In January 1863, he issued his famous Emancipation Proclamation, freeing the slaves in the rebellion states.

President Lincoln visits Union troops during the Civil War (above). The Lincoln penny (right) was first minted in 1909.

The tide began to turn in favor of the Union, which had also begun enlisting black soldiers—men literally fighting for their freedom. On April 9, 1865, the last of the southern forces surrendered. The war had lasted four years and cost more than 600,000 lives.

A NATION MOURNS

Lincoln had seen the country through its worst period and helped to preserve it. He had won a second term as president in 1864 and focused on reconstructing the war-shattered South "with malice toward none; with charity for all." He also called for better treatment of black people in America, including the right to vote.

The Civil War had made Lincoln many enemies. Less than a week after the South's surrender, a Confederate sympathizer fatally shot the president at close range in Ford's Theatre in Washington, D.C. Freed slaves lined the streets of Lincoln's funeral parade to pay their respects to the Great Emancipator. The 13th Amendment to the Constitution was ratified at the end of 1865, outlawing slavery in the United States.

Lincoln is shot at Ford's Theatre on April 14, 1865.

WHITE HOUSE HEROES
INSPIRING U.S. PRESIDENTS

Arguably the most powerful person in the world, the president of the United States is not only a leader, but also a human being who sometimes makes controversial or unpopular decisions. The four featured here stand out for their influential administrations.

32ND U.S. PRESIDENT: Franklin D. Roosevelt
(1882–1945); Term: 1933–1945

Better known as FDR, this charismatic, aristocratic former governor of New York led the United States through the Great Depression—a decade of economic crisis triggered by the epic 1929 crash of the stock market. Through New Deal economic policies that aimed to help the unemployed and to enable businesses and agriculture to recover, and by working with America's allies during World War II, President Roosevelt achieved victory at home and in the war.

INSPIRING WORDS: "The test of our progress is not whether we add more to the abundance of those who have much; it is whether we provide enough for those who have too little."

35TH U.S. PRESIDENT: John F. Kennedy
(1917–1963); Term: 1961–1963

The youngest president ever elected, JFK served at a crucial time during the Cold War—a period of intense superpower rivalry between the United States and the former Soviet Union—and the height of the civil rights movement, which he helped by championing laws against the discrimination of black people. Kennedy's skills at international negotiation prevented the Soviet Union from building missile bases in Cuba, while narrowly sparing the world from a nuclear war. He also revved up the U.S.–Soviet race to explore space before his assassination, at the age of 46.

INSPIRING WORDS: "Ask not what your country can do for you. Ask what you can do for your country."

40TH U.S. PRESIDENT: Ronald Reagan

(1911–2004); Term: 1981–1989

Before he became governor of California, U.S.A., and later a two-term president of the United States, Ronald Reagan was an actor in more than 50 films. He brought that camera-ready persona to the Oval Office. Americans who prefer fewer social services in exchange for smaller government celebrate Reagan as their hero. He took a hard stance against the Soviet Union during the Cold War but relied on diplomacy—words rather than war—to reduce nuclear weapons in both countries. In 1987, he famously challenged Soviet leader Mikhail Gorbachev to take down the wall separating Soviet-occupied East Berlin from West Berlin. (The Berlin Wall symbolized the Iron Curtain between Western Europe and the communist states of Eastern Europe during the Cold War.) Two years later, the wall came down. The Cold War was over.

INSPIRING WORDS: "Mr. Gorbachev, tear down this wall!"

44TH U.S. PRESIDENT: Barack Obama

(1961–); Term: 2009–2017

Barack Obama worked as a civil rights lawyer, community organizer, and constitutional law teacher before entering politics and becoming the first black president of the United States. He guided the nation through a worldwide economic crisis and two wars abroad while battling stiff opposition from the opposing political party. He also championed a number of beneficial yet controversial policies, including affordable health care for all Americans, marriage rights for gay people, and the need to address climate change.

INSPIRING WORDS: "Change will not come if we wait for some other person or some other time."

GUTSY GALS

PHENOMENAL FIRST LADY:
Eleanor Roosevelt (1884–1962)

Eleanor Roosevelt, wife of U.S. president Franklin D. Roosevelt, was a first lady of many firsts. She held the first ever press conferences given by a president's wife—more than 300 of them. She authored books and wrote a column called My Day about her opinions on social and political issues. And at a time when few married women had careers, Eleanor surprised many when she matched the president's yearly salary, earning $75,000 from lecturing and writing (she donated most of her earnings to charity). She also used her position to give a voice to people who didn't have one: women, children, African Americans, and the poor. Eleanor changed the role of the first lady forever—and for the better.

KING TUT

ANCIENT EGYPT'S MVP (MOST VALUABLE PHARAOH)

No one knows how Tutankhamun felt the day he was crowned Egypt's pharaoh—or king—in 1334 B.C. Was he excited to have the army at his command? Did he feel empowered by his ability to create laws? Was he nervous about talking to the gods?

Such mixed emotions were only natural: Being pharaoh was a big job for a nine-year-old.

Tutankhamun, aka King Tut, wasn't the first boy king to rule ancient Egypt, but he is the most famous. His rock-cut burial chamber in the hidden Valley of the Kings is unique in that it hadn't been emptied by thieves. Instead, it sat largely undisturbed for more than three millennia until Egyptologist Howard Carter discovered its front door buried beneath ancient worker huts, in 1922. As Carter peered through a tiny hole in the door, a companion asked if he could see anything. "Yes," Carter said. "Wonderful things!"

The four chambers of King Tut's tomb contained more than 5,000 artifacts, from a simple fire-starting gizmo to a golden throne. The most valuable object was Tut's mummy. Egyptologists know few details of the boy king's reign, except that it was brief—less than ten years—and that it ended abruptly with his mysterious death. Modern technologies revealed that he was in poor health, unable to walk without a cane and weakened by a disease called malaria. Scientists continue to probe the mummy for clues about his death, while his trove of treasures teaches us about life in that ancient kingdom on the Nile.

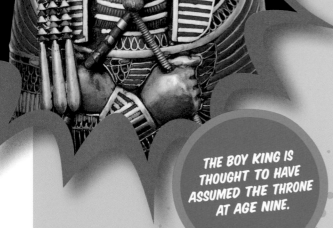

THE BOY KING IS THOUGHT TO HAVE ASSUMED THE THRONE AT AGE NINE.

FEARLESS FACTS

➔ **BORN:** ca 1341 B.C., ancient Egypt ➔ **DIED:** ca 1323 B.C., ancient Egypt
➔ **OCCUPATION:** Pharaoh ➔ **BOLDEST MOMENT:** Becoming king of Egypt at the age of nine

ALEXANDER THE GREAT

How's this for some cool schooling: Your gym class covers sword fighting, archery, and horseback riding. During recess, you pretend you're Achilles, the Greek superhero, in a game invented by your math teacher. After lunch, you take lessons in history, literature, and drama from Aristotle, the famous philosopher. Welcome to the Class of 343 B.C., an exclusive school with a student body of one. His name was Alexander II, and he was the future ruler of the Greek kingdom of Macedonia and eventually an empire that spanned three continents. Alexander lived a short life, but he accomplished more in just a few years than most leaders achieve during their entire lives.

Alexander the Great, one of history's greatest military commanders, left home for his first battle when he was only 17. He teamed up with his dad, King Philip II of Macedonia, to unite nearly all of Greece's independent states—a feat he had to repeat two years later when his father was assassinated. With all of Greece united and under his control, young King Alexander II set a bigger challenge: building an empire.

Alexander led by example, boldly charging into battle at the head of his armies—even against overwhelming odds. In eight years, Alexander conquered the Persian Empire, Egypt (which he ruled as a pharaoh), parts of what would become Iran and Iraq, and India. Along the way, he spread Greek culture, language, art, and architecture, while taking on the customs of his diverse subjects. For a brief time, Alexander ruled the world's largest empire. Today, more than 20 cities—including Alexandria, Egypt—bear his name.

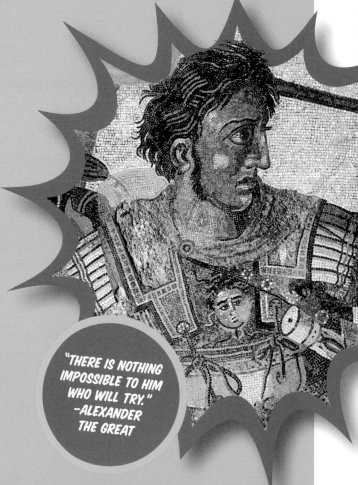

"THERE IS NOTHING IMPOSSIBLE TO HIM WHO WILL TRY."
—ALEXANDER THE GREAT

FEARLESS FACTS

➔ **BORN:** July 356 B.C., Macedonia ➔ **DIED:** June 323 B.C. Babylon ➔ **OCCUPATION:** General, king
➔ **BOLDEST MOMENT:** He united all of ancient Greece's squabbling states—twice!

BEATING THE ODDS
FOUR DARING LEADERS

When situations seemed hopeless and defeat was not an option, these courageous commanders relied on their smarts, strategy, and grit to turn the tide of battle. See how they led their armies—and nations—through their most desperate times.

FIGHTING FOUNDING FATHER:
George Washington (1732–1799)

Dodging floating chunks of ice in the dark and paddling through bone-chilling sleet, General George Washington led his force of roughly 2,400 Continental Army soldiers across the freezing Delaware River from Pennsylvania, U.S.A., to New Jersey, U.S.A., on Christmas night 1776. The general was desperate for a victory in the war for independence from England. He needed to inspire his troops—many of them dressed in rags and weary from defeat—and he thought a surprise attack via this dangerous route might catch the enemy off guard.

His tactic worked. Washington's men surprised and defeated an encampment of British-paid German mercenaries in Trenton, New Jersey. Although this victory was a small one, it boosted morale and recruitment for the Continental Army. It was just another example of Washington's trademark daring and leadership skills. (To read more about Washington, turn the page.)

IN BRITAIN'S FINEST HOUR:
Winston Churchill (1874–1965)

"The Battle of France is over," English prime minister Winston Churchill told the British House of Commons in 1940. "I expect the Battle of Britain is about to begin." The defeated French had just signed a cease-fire with Germany, leaving Britain on its own to face the full military might of Nazi Germany near the start of World War II. The Germans had conquered most of Western Europe in a short amount of time. Churchill was determined that Britain wouldn't be next. He rallied his countrymen through the force of his personality, delivering some of history's most inspiring speeches in a defiant voice. The Battle of Britain—the world's first all-air battle—commenced that summer.

THE MAGIC TOUCH: Horatio Nelson
(1758–1805)

"Beat to quarters!" Sailors scurry barefoot on decks that have been covered with sand to sop up blood from the battle to come. *Ka-chunk! Ka-chunk! Ka-chunk!* Gunports swing open and crews heave cannons into position as kid crew members called powder monkeys scurry belowdecks for ammunition. Amid the action, Vice Admiral Horatio Nelson strolls calmly beneath clouds of sails on the quarterdeck of the H.M.S. *Victory*, his 104-cannon flagship. Thirty-three warships of the French and Spanish fleets— England's enemies in 1805— have sailed out to engage Nelson's 27 ships off of Spain's Cape Trafalgar. If Nelson loses this battle, little will stand between French Emperor Napoleon Bonaparte and his conquest of Britain.

Although small in stature, Nelson looms large in England's history as one of its greatest heroes. He went to sea at 12 and became a captain at 20. By 1805, the vice admiral had lost an arm and an eye in previous bouts of heroics. He brought to each battle an unpredictable style of strategy: the Nelson Touch. It was on display at Trafalgar. Instead of sailing his ships in a line parallel to the enemy vessels and blasting them with broadsides—standard procedure in Napoleonic-era sea combat—Nelson ordered his fleet to break through the enemy's line and sink as many ships as possible. The tactic worked, but at a great cost. Refusing to cover his uniform's rank insignias—bull's-eyes for enemy sharpshooters—Nelson was shot by a sniper in the rigging of a French ship. England's savior lived long enough to see the enemy surrender. The H.M.S. *Victory*'s log recorded his final words: "Thank God I have done my duty."

GUTSY GALS

WARRIOR QUEEN: Artemisia (ca 500 B.C.)

After her husband the king died, Artemisia took over the throne and led the people of Halicarnassus— then part of the Persian Empire— into war against the Greeks, proving herself as a cunning military leader. In 480 B.C., she personally commanded five ships in the Persian War's Battle of Salamis. Though her side lost the battle, the clever queen saved her ship by taking down her flags and ramming a passing Persian vessel. Fooled into thinking she was on their side, the Greeks let Artemisia and her crew escape to fight again.

Wave after wave of German fighter planes and bombers clashed with Royal Air Force fighters in the skies over England. British Spitfire and German Bf 109 aircraft fell to earth riddled with bullet holes and trailing smoke as British citizens hid in bomb shelters. Churchill kept up morale and pressed for defense, despite overwhelming odds (at the height of the battle, Germany possessed nearly four times as many combat aircraft). After three months of constant air combat, the Royal Air Force emerged victorious. "Never in the field of human conflict was so much owed by so many to so few," Churchill said of his country's brave pilots.

YOU DON'T KNOW
GEORGE

Washington's dentures

FASCINATING FACTS ABOUT AMERICA'S FOUNDING FATHER...

Greatest American hero. A general who led a ragtag army to victory against the most fearsome military in the world. Model president. What more can be said about George Washington that you haven't heard already in history class? Turns out, there's plenty...

WASHINGTON DIDN'T DO SOME OF THE THINGS YOU THINK HE DID.

You know that tale about young George Washington cutting down a cherry tree and then admitting the misdeed to his dad? Or the time he chucked a silver dollar across the Potomac River? Those stories are just that—stories! (They were myths created shortly after Washington's death.) He didn't have wooden teeth, either, although he did suffer from dental problems his entire life and wore a variety of dental appliances made of gold, human teeth, hippopotamus ivory, and brass screws.

WASHINGTON WAS LUCKY AS WELL AS PLUCKY.

Washington's legendary courage on the battlefield got him into many close scrapes throughout his military career. During the Revolutionary War, he led his troops to within 30 yards (27 m) of the enemy, then stood firm as both sides opened fire. When the smoke cleared, Washington sat tall atop his horse, sword drawn and unhurt. Long before the war for independence in America, when young Washington was a volunteer in the British Army, he survived a disastrous ambush in one of the early battles of the French and Indian War. He survived the retreat with four bullet holes in his coat and two horses shot out beneath him. One Native American chief who shot at Washington swore he was protected by supernatural powers.

Washington at Valley Forge, Pennsylvania, U.S.A.

WASHINGTON DID A LOT OF THINGS YOU DIDN'T KNOW HE DID.

Before he became a military man, statesman, and president, young Washington grew tobacco on his family's land at Mount Vernon, Virginia, U.S.A. He left school at 15 to work as a surveyor, mapping the land around his county. (These terrain-charting skills served him well later in life as a general.) Washington was also an excellent horseman and dancer, although he was self-conscious about his lack of a college education (the other major Founding Fathers all attended prestigious schools). Later in life, Washington bred hounds with names like Venus and Sweet Lips, dabbled in architecture, and ran his own distillery.

WASHINGTON LOST MORE BATTLES THAN HE WON.

Washington lacked experience leading a large force when he was appointed as commander in chief of the Continental Army, and he made several strategic mistakes during the war. But that doesn't mean he was a lousy general. A natural leader, Washington looked after the needs of his ragged army, retreated when necessary, and stoked their fighting spirit. His trademark luck turned some blunders into victories. And his decision to inoculate his troops against deadly smallpox—which Washington had survived as a child, and was therefore immune to—may have been the smartest strategic decision of the Revolutionary War.

WASHINGTON DIDN'T WANT TO BE PRESIDENT.

After winning the war for America, Washington wanted nothing more than to return to a peaceful life at Mount Vernon, but the nation still needed him. The Founding Fathers were at odds over how the new government should be set up, and only Washington—the young republic's greatest hero—commanded enough respect to bring about compromise. He was the unanimous choice for the country's first president. Once in office, he treated the job with respect and seriousness, well aware that history would be watching. He established a cabinet of the country's smartest people and listened to their advice. He avoided any trappings—such as titles or clothing—that would draw comparisons to a king. Although he could easily have won another election, he turned down a third term and retired to Mount Vernon, setting a high standard for all presidents to come.

Mount Vernon

19

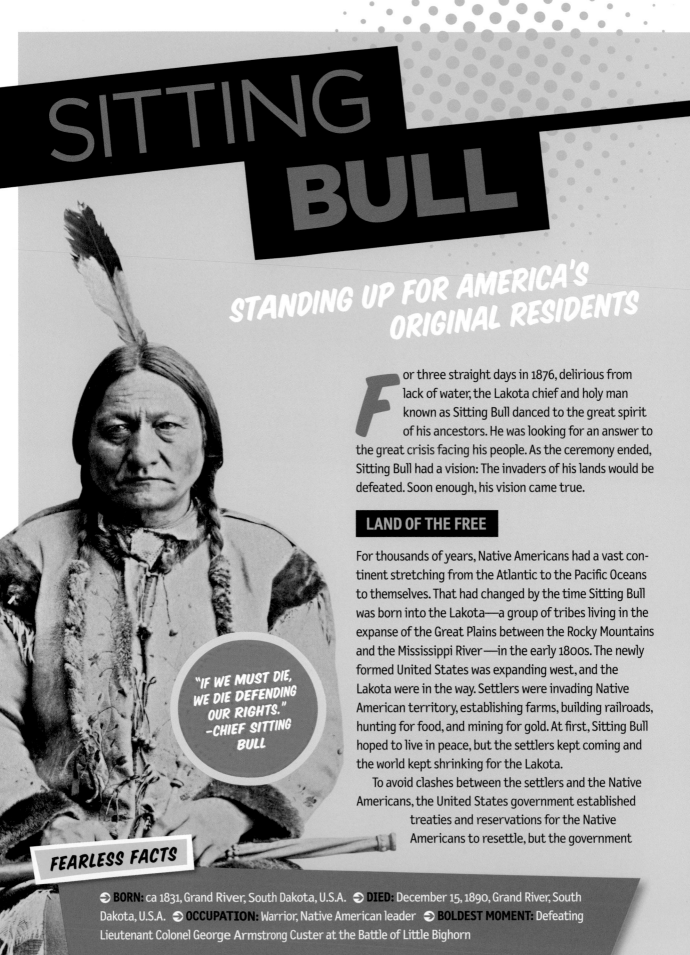

SITTING BULL

STANDING UP FOR AMERICA'S ORIGINAL RESIDENTS

For three straight days in 1876, delirious from lack of water, the Lakota chief and holy man known as Sitting Bull danced to the great spirit of his ancestors. He was looking for an answer to the great crisis facing his people. As the ceremony ended, Sitting Bull had a vision: The invaders of his lands would be defeated. Soon enough, his vision came true.

LAND OF THE FREE

For thousands of years, Native Americans had a vast continent stretching from the Atlantic to the Pacific Oceans to themselves. That had changed by the time Sitting Bull was born into the Lakota—a group of tribes living in the expanse of the Great Plains between the Rocky Mountains and the Mississippi River—in the early 1800s. The newly formed United States was expanding west, and the Lakota were in the way. Settlers were invading Native American territory, establishing farms, building railroads, hunting for food, and mining for gold. At first, Sitting Bull hoped to live in peace, but the settlers kept coming and the world kept shrinking for the Lakota.

To avoid clashes between the settlers and the Native Americans, the United States government established treaties and reservations for the Native Americans to resettle, but the government

"IF WE MUST DIE, WE DIE DEFENDING OUR RIGHTS."
-CHIEF SITTING BULL

FEARLESS FACTS

➡ **BORN:** ca 1831, Grand River, South Dakota, U.S.A. ➡ **DIED:** December 15, 1890, Grand River, South Dakota, U.S.A. ➡ **OCCUPATION:** Warrior, Native American leader ➡ **BOLDEST MOMENT:** Defeating Lieutenant Colonel George Armstrong Custer at the Battle of Little Bighorn

often broke its promises and reservations were harsh places to live. Overhunting by settlers left the Native Americans without food and forced them to depend on the United States for help. By the 1860s, Sitting Bull had had enough. He began to fight back.

CHIEF OF CHIEFS

Sitting Bull killed his first buffalo at 10 and clobbered an enemy in a rival clan at 14. But he was compassionate as well as courageous, and was chosen to lead a group that looked after the welfare of his people. He refused to compromise when it came to the well-being of the Lakota. He took up arms against American soldiers in the 1860s, hoping to frighten settlers away from his land. He was soon made the supreme chief of all the Lakota and other tribes living in the Great Plains.

GOLD RUSH

The discovery of gold brought a flood of settlers to sacred Native American land in the 1870s. Breaking its own treaties, the American government declared war on any Native Americans who refused to live on reservations. Thousands flocked to follow Sitting Bull—who refused to sign any treaties with the U.S. government—at his camp near the Little Bighorn River in what is now Montana. When Lt. Col. George Armstrong Custer and his troops attacked the camp, Sitting Bull's warriors wiped them out in a battle that would become a famous defeat for the U.S. Army. The vision from Sitting Bull's dancing ceremony had come to pass. But victory was short-lived. The Army struck back with greater numbers, and it became clear that Native Americans couldn't stand against the rising tide of white settlers. Sitting Bull was forced to flee with his people to Canada.

His life took a surprising twist in 1884 when he met and befriended sharpshooting legend Annie Oakley, star of Buffalo Bill Cody's Wild West show (see sidebar). Sitting Bull toured with the show as an ambassador of the Lakota. He became a celebrity and icon of the American West, defending his people until the end of his life.

Sitting Bull with Buffalo Bill Cody (above); tepees at the camp of Sitting Bull, in South Dakota (left)

BOLD BOSSES
HERO CEOS

THE OPTIMISTIC GENIUS: Elon Musk (1971–)

He's a billionaire genius who flies his own jet, has a race car, and invests in everything from spaceships to alternate-energy resources. If you think that sounds like Tony Stark, alter-ego of Iron Man, you're half right. Actor Robert Downey, Jr., based his movie portrayal of Tony Stark on Elon Musk, the real-life South African–born whiz kid who struck it rich in Internet startups before investing in his real passion: technologies for a better future.

Musk's SpaceX company builds rockets to reach Earth's orbit and beyond. (He plans to eventually colonize Mars!) His Tesla company builds electric cars that go farther and faster on a single charge without burning a drop of gasoline—better than clunkier previous models. He co-founded SolarCity to make sun-fueled energy systems for houses and cities, helping residents rely less on fossil fuels. It's an ambitious collection of companies for a man who could have retired after making his first billion. Musk is investing in a brighter tomorrow for everyone—or at least finding us another planet to live on if things here don't work out.

THE BENEVOLENT BILLIONAIRE: Bill Gates (1955–)

This computer whiz co-founded Microsoft and in 1985 pioneered the Windows operating system, which was easier to use than the clunky interfaces of the day. His software transformed computers from business machines into essential desktop devices for work and fun. Gates soon accomplished his mission of putting a personal computer in nearly every home in America.

In the process, Gates became one of the richest men in the world—and then started giving his money away. Along with his wife, he donated $30 billion to form the Bill & Melinda Gates Foundation, which works to improve education, water quality, and sanitation across the world. Along with fellow billionaire CEO Warren Buffett, Gates started the Giving Pledge, a challenge to the world's wealthiest people to donate at least half of their fortunes to charitable causes. So far, more than 130 billionaires have signed the pledge.

THE HIP-HOP HERO: Russell Simmons (1957–)

Music moguls are famous for their lavish lifestyles—living in sprawling mansions, driving fancy cars, hanging out with famous friends—and Russell Simmons is no different. As one of the founders of Def Jam Recordings, he kick-started the careers of some of rap's biggest stars, from Will Smith to the Beastie Boys to LL Cool J, before selling his company for a fortune. But when he puts the music on pause, Simmons focuses on causes for the greater good. He manages a foundation that promotes better relations between Jewish, black, and Muslim people, and he also advocates for gay rights.

Simmons started Rush Communications, one of the largest black-owned media companies in the United States. Along with his two brothers, Simmons founded the Rush Philanthropic Arts Foundation to bring music education to kids whose families can't afford it otherwise. Music has been good to Simmons; now he wants to share it.

THE SOCIAL NETWORKER: Mark Zuckerberg (1984–)

As a kid growing up outside New York City, young Mark Zuckerberg preferred making video games to playing them. He created an instant-messaging program called ZuckNet just for his family members and a cool media player that learned to play songs based on the listener's habits. But those apps were child's play compared to Facebook, the social network he launched with his roommates at Harvard University in 2004. Zuckerberg had poured all of his time and energy into creating the site. Facebook made him his first billion before his 24th birthday. Today he's worth more than $45 billion.

Zuckerberg hopes his site brings people around the world closer together with each shared comment, photo, and "liked" post. And like his hero Bill Gates, Zuckerberg has pledged to donate most of his wealth—99 percent of his Facebook stock—to charities over his lifetime. He's off to a good start. Zuckerberg (whose annual salary at Facebook is one dollar) has given more than a billion dollars to a variety of causes, from education to the battle against the deadly Ebola virus in Africa.

TALK SHOW SUPERSTAR: Oprah Winfrey (1954–)

GUTSY GALS

Born into extreme poverty, young Oprah Winfrey sometimes had to wear potato sacks because her family couldn't afford clothes. Today, she's worth an estimated three billion dollars and is the only black woman on *Forbes*'s list of the 400 richest people in America. Winfrey succeeded through sheer determination. When she was fired less than eight months after starting a job as the first black female news anchor at WTVF in Nashville, Tennessee, U.S.A., Winfrey didn't let it keep her down. In 1983, she started working at *A.M. Chicago*, the lowest-rated talk show in Chicago—and within a month turned it into the highest-rated one. Three years later, its name was changed to *The Oprah Winfrey Show*. Winfrey's warm-hearted personality earned her loyal fans, and the show aired for 25 seasons, from 1986 to 2011, making it one of the longest running daytime television shows in history.

KING LEONIDAS

DEFENDING TO THE END

"COME AND TAKE THEM!" —KING LEONIDAS, IN RESPONSE TO A DEMAND TO LAY DOWN HIS ARMS

"Hand over your [weapons]," demanded Xerxes I, king of the first Persian Empire, as his armies prepared to invade the Greek city-state of Sparta. "Come and take them," answered Leonidas, Sparta's legendary king. His fighting words launched one of history's most lopsided battles. The Persian king unleashed as many as 150,000 troops against Leonidas's army of 300, aided by a few hundred soldiers from other city-states. Leonidas took only older soldiers who had at least one son at home. He doubted his men would survive the coming battle.

But if any army could overcome overwhelming odds, it was Sparta's. Along with every other man in this city-state, Leonidas was trained for battle since the age of 7, when he was enrolled into a brutal military school called the Agoge. It was like the world's worst summer camp—one that lasted year-round. Young Leonidas was barely fed, forced to sleep outside, and trained how to wield weapons and fight. Any boys who couldn't handle life in the Agoge grew up to be second-class citizens. Graduates joined the army at 20 and defended Sparta for life.

Spartans fought in a fearsome formation called a phalanx. The warriors stood shoulder to shoulder, several men deep, linking their shields to form a moving wall of metal and flicking spearheads. Using this tactic, the Spartans were able to hold off Xerxes' thousands in a narrow mountain pass known as the Hot Gates. They were eventually overrun, but tales of Spartan courage have echoed through history as an example of men who never give up. It's no wonder the Spartans believed they were descendants of Hercules, buff hero of Greek mythology.

FEARLESS FACTS

➔ **BORN:** ca 540 B.C., Sparta ➔ **DIED:** 480 B.C., Thermopylae ➔ **OCCUPATION:** King
➔ **BOLDEST MOMENT:** Leading just 300 Spartan soldiers in battle against tens of thousands of invaders

WILLIAM WALLACE

Mounted on mighty warhorses, more than 300 English cavalrymen approached a narrow wooden bridge near the Scottish village of Stirling in the fall of 1297. These were the most fearsome warriors of their time, sent to put down a rebellion led by one man: William Wallace. Once an independent kingdom, Scotland was now under the rule of England's King Edward I, who had snatched control of the country when Scotland's previous king had died. Wallace was unhappy with how his countrymen were taxed and mistreated under the English regime. He picked a fight with England's king to restore Scottish independence.

At what would become known as the Battle of Stirling Bridge, Wallace commanded his men to hold back as England's mounted warriors and infantrymen crossed the bridge in pairs. Hours passed, and yet Wallace urged patience. Then, when about half of England's forces were on his side of the river, Wallace gave the signal. Attack! Wielding spears, the Scottish soldiers pressed the English cavalry and infantrymen back to the river. The mighty mounted soldiers floundered and panicked as they were pushed into the water or separated from their comrades.

After this humiliating defeat for the English, Wallace was knighted and named Guardian of Scotland, a title with powers similar to a king's. He was later captured by the English and accused of treason, but Wallace denied the charges to his dying breath. Scotland eventually gained its independence, and Wallace is one of the country's greatest heroes.

"I CANNOT BE A TRAITOR, FOR I OWE HIM NO ALLEGIANCE." —WILLIAM WALLACE, REFERRING TO ENGLAND'S KING

FEARLESS FACTS

➔ **BORN:** ca 1270, Scotland   ➔ **DIED:** August 1305, England   ➔ **OCCUPATION:** Scottish knight
➔ **BOLDEST MOMENT:** Defeating mounted English knights with a much smaller force of Scottish infantry

MOMENT OF BRAVERY

This superhero mayor was called to action above and beyond the duties of his office. How did he answer?

THE SITUATION

Cory Booker arrived home one evening in April 2012 to a terrifying sight: His neighbor's house was on fire! Although the fire department had been called, firefighters hadn't arrived yet, so Booker rushed into the building to make sure no one was inside. He found a sleeping man and shook him awake, telling him to head to the door. The smell of smoke was overpowering; the fire seemed to have started upstairs. Then Booker heard a woman screaming, "I'm here. I'm here. Help!" He ran up the stairs to see flames licking up the walls. Smoke filled the hallway, making it hard to breathe and even harder to see. Booker was about to head toward the woman's panicked voice when a bodyguard grabbed him by the belt and stopped him from going farther.

THE MOMENT OF TRUTH

Cory Booker was not just a concerned neighbor. He was the mayor of this city: Newark, New Jersey, U.S.A. His security team—men charged with protecting him—had followed him into the burning house. Booker's job as the mayor came with big responsibilities, and he couldn't endanger his life recklessly. But the woman calling for help was also one of his constituents, a citizen of his city. Booker wanted to save her. His bodyguard told him it was too dangerous to go any farther.

But Booker had a history of helping others. Before he was mayor, as a city council member, he camped in a crime-ridden section of the city to call attention to its problems and push for increased police patrols. During a 2010 blizzard, he grabbed a shovel and cleared snow from residents' cars and sidewalks. He once helped a pedestrian hit by a car. He even saved a freezing dog that was trapped outside in a storm.

So naturally the superhero mayor, as he'd come to be known on social media, ran into the burning house to help his neighbors. He ordered his bodyguard to let him go and pressed deeper into the smoke, which was so thick that Booker could barely see. It was getting harder to breathe, too. He finally found the 48-year-old woman lying in bed. Booker, a tall and burly former college football player, hoisted the woman over his shoulder and headed for the exit. He passed through the kitchen, where the flames spread across the ceiling. Embers and ash rained down, singeing his skin. Booker began coughing from the smoke. When he reached the stairs, his bodyguard helped him carry the woman to the ground floor and through the front door. They had rescued everyone in the burning building.

THE LEGACY

When firefighters arrived at the house, they found Mayor Booker hunched over and struggling to catch his breath. He and the woman he saved were taken to the hospital and treated for smoke inhalation and second-degree burns from the falling embers. The woman made a full recovery. "I did what any neighbor would do—help a neighbor," Booker said at a press conference the next day. In 2013, the superhero mayor ended his service in Newark's highest office. He was elected to the U.S. Senate.

CHAPTER TWO

LEGENDARY LADS

Don't look for all of this chapter's heroes in the history books. They live in a realm between the real world and legend, in songs and poems and campfire stories that grow larger with each telling. From Hercules to Robin Hood to their more modern counterparts, you'll meet the men (and women) behind the myths. Some tales are true, others are pure fantasy, but all the heroes here have big hearts and lots of guts—even if they never existed in flesh and blood.

Boy wizard Harry Potter takes aim at the bad guys.

ROBIN HOOD

THE ORIGINAL OUTLAW WITH A HEART OF GOLD

"WE NEVER ROB. WE JUST SORT OF BORROW A BIT FROM THOSE WHO CAN AFFORD IT." —ROBIN HOOD TO LITTLE JOHN IN THE 1973 DISNEY FILM ROBIN HOOD

A grove of trees shades an ancient grave in the countryside of northern England, near the River Calder and the crumbling gatehouse of a ruined nunnery. Faded and green with moss, the grave's marker bears an inscription that has intrigued travelers and historians for centuries: "Here underneath this little stone, lies Robert Earl of Huntingdon. Never was there an archer as good, and people called him Robin Hood." Could this serene spot mark the resting place of the most famous outlaw who ever lived? That is, if Robin Hood ever lived at all.

BALLADS TO BLOCKBUSTERS

From today going back to the 14th century, movie directors, poets, and singers of stories called ballads have built upon the famous tale of an outlaw archer who prowled Sherwood Forest with his band of Merry Men. From their hideout at the Major Oak—a sprawling tree that still stands today near the village of Edwinstowe—Robin and his gang staged raids on the well-to-do and split their loot with the downtrodden, always one step ahead of the corrupt Sheriff of Nottingham. Clad in dark green duds to blend with forest shadows, Robin Hood was a supernatural shot with his

FEARLESS FACTS

→ **BORN:** Possibly in the late 12th century, Loxley, England → **DIED:** Possibly in the mid-13th century, West Yorkshire, England → **OCCUPATION:** Archer, outlaw → **BOLDEST MOMENT:** Outsmarting the dastardly Sheriff of Nottingham

bow and arrow, able to split a tree branch from 300 yards (274 m) away.

He also connected with ordinary working people in medieval times, when kings and their nobles ruled over the peasants who did all the work. In the earliest versions of his story, Robin Hood was a commoner who caused all sorts of grief for the greedy landowners and their lackeys. In later ballads, Robin Hood was a loyal fighter for England's King Richard the Lionheart, whose corrupt brother declared Robin an outlaw while the king was away.

THE REAL ROBYN HODE

But is either version based on a real guy? Medieval scholars didn't doubt that Robin Hood was based on a real outlaw, but modern historians say the names and dates don't add up. The city of Nottingham, for instance, didn't begin appointing sheriffs until centuries after Robin Hood's reign as the prince of thieves. Scientific tests of the Major Oak tree show that it would have been just a sapling when the Merry Men supposedly built a hideout in its branches.

Records going back to the 13th century do contain the names "Robert Hood," "Robyn Hode," "Robehod," and similar variations. But bandits were often given the nickname Robynhood and the like as a sign of their criminal status. Whether a real-life outlaw inspired the nicknames or the nicknames inspired the legend, historians have no way of knowing.

A GRAVE ERROR?

Even the final resting place of Robin Hood raises more questions than it answers. According to the ballads, Robin Hood died after he was betrayed by a trusted friend at the Kirklees Priory, a nunnery near the River Calder. Weakened by poison, Hood uttered his dying words to his companion Little John. "Bury me where my arrow falls," Robin said, as he fired one final shot from the nunnery's gatehouse. The grave beneath the grove, however, lies outside of bow range—at least outside the bow range of an ordinary medieval archer. But if the ballads are to be believed, history's most famous thief was far from ordinary. "Such outlaws as him and his men," reads the faded final line on his grave, "England will never see again."

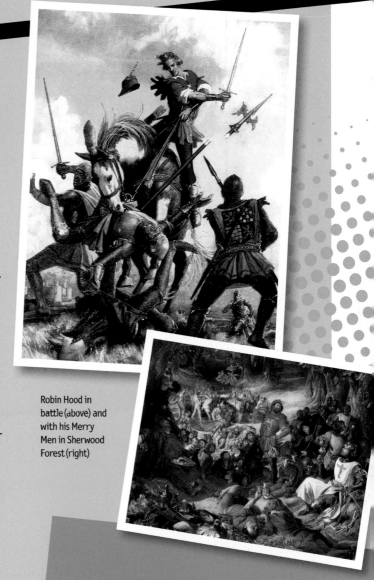

Robin Hood in battle (above) and with his Merry Men in Sherwood Forest (right)

USUAL SUSPECTS: WAS ONE OF THESE MEN THE REAL ROBIN HOOD?

➲ ROBERT HOD OF YORK: Records from 1226 contain the earliest reference to a man named Robert Hod, who turned outlaw after his money was seized for taxes.

➲ ROBIN OF LOXLEY: A tale from around 1600 claims Robin Hood was born in Loxley, Warwickshire, and became a knight before turning outlaw.

➲ THE EARL OF HUNTINGDON: This ally of King Richard is outed as Robin Hood in a 17th-century ballad. He is also named on Robin Hood's supposed grave.

ROGUES' GALLERY
GOOD BAD GUYS

Robin Hood is hardly the only folk hero who accomplished heroic deeds while lurking on the wrong side of the law. Meet some legendary lawbreakers—including a bandit, a gunslinger, and even a pirate—in this roundup of rapscallions.

REVOLUTIONARY LEADER: Pancho Villa (1878–1923)

José Doroteo Arango Arámbula—better known by his nickname Pancho Villa—was in front of a firing squad in 1912 for allegedly stealing horses when he persuaded his captors to spare his life just minutes before his execution. It was just one of many amazing moments in the charmed life of this smooth-talking Mexican folk hero, who turned outlaw as a teenager after dispatching a man who was harassing his sister.

Villa's band of thieves robbed only from the rich, making him a hero to the poor. His outlaw skills served Villa well when he joined the revolution against Mexican dictator Porfirio Díaz in 1910. Villa's exploits as a revolutionary leader—charging headlong into battle with his men—were captured on early movie cameras, turning the dashing bandit turned revolutionary into an international celebrity.

LEGENDARY LAWMAN: Wyatt Earp (1848–1929)

The most famous gunfight of the American West ended just 30 seconds after the first shots rang out. When the smoke cleared near the O.K. Corral in the frontier town of Tombstone, Arizona, U.S.A., one man was left unscathed: Marshall Wyatt Earp. Along with his two brothers and fellow lawman John Henry "Doc" Holliday, Earp had defeated four notorious outlaws, imposing some order on the mostly lawless expanse of the Wild West in the 1880s.

Earp turned to law enforcement after his wife died in 1870. Aimless and hardly an angel himself (he once stole a horse), Earp settled in the mining boomtown of Tombstone to help his brothers find their fortune in gold. That fortune never came, so Earp turned to taming the ruthless cowboy gang that terrorized the countryside. His shootout at the O.K. Corral cemented Earp's reputation as a legend of the American West.

PRINCE OF PIRATES: Samuel Bellamy (1689–1717)

"Pirate ho!" The sight of a mysterious ship flying a black flag put a lump in the throats of 17th-century merchant sea captains. Real-life pirates were blood-thirsty bandits of the ocean during the Golden Age of Piracy (from the late 1600s to the early 1700s), and merchant sailors who came under buccaneer attack had two options: surrender or die.

Unless the pirate was Captain Samuel Bellamy, aka Black Sam. This dashing English captain had a reputation for going easy on his captives and treating his crew like equals. Sailors knew him as the Prince of Pirates, a title Bellamy relished. But he also saw himself as a sort of high-seas Robin Hood: a bandit robbing from rich merchants and spreading the wealth among his working-class crewmen—many of them former slaves. "[The merchants] rob the poor under the cover of law," Bellamy once lectured the captain of a captured ship, "and we plunder the rich under the protection of our own courage." Flying the skull-and-crossbones, the Prince of Pirates plundered more than 50 ships, becoming the wealthi-est pirate of the 18th century.

OUT OF THE SHADOWS: Hattori Hanzō (1542–1596)

At twilight in the 16th-century Japanese countryside, merce-naries clad in black slid from shadow to shadow, carrying with them all the weapons and tools necessary for dangerous duty. They were ninjas—also known as *shinobi*—trained since childhood in the arts of stealth, espionage, and assassination. Like all men and women who entered this sinister trade, ninjas were feared and despised for their sneaky tactics.

But when hundreds of power-hungry warlords squabbled over control of Japan in the 1500s, a ninja named Hattori Hanzō emerged from the shadows to help unite the coun-try. He rescued the daughters of the warlord Tokugawa Ieyasu and later led them to safety across the countryside, with the help of his ninja clan. When Ieyasu took control of Japan from the warlords, Hanzō became known as Devil Hanzō for his skill and supposed supernatural abilities.

PIRATE QUEEN: Anne Bonny (ca 1698–1782)

GUTSY GALS

It was an old sailor's saying that a woman on a ship brought bad luck—but not if the ship was a pirate ship and the woman was Anne Bonny. The Irish-born Bonny fell in love with a pirate named John "Calico Jack" Rackham and joined his crew for a life on the high seas. Legend says she began her pirating career by cleverly tricking a passing merchant ship into giving up its goods by using a fake corpse she'd made with a mannequin and some fake blood. When the ship's crew saw Bonny standing over her "victim," they surrendered without a fight. Most of the time, Bonny dressed as a woman. But she found that skirts got in the way of pillaging and plundering, so when it was time for piracy, the pirate queen would forgo her dresses for pants.

JACQUES PORTEFAIX

THE BOY WHO CRIED WEREWOLF

The landscape of southern France looked straight out of a fairy tale in the 1700s, dotted with medieval hamlets and covered in hilly forests. But across this fantasy landscape prowled a real monster. Hunters swore that bullets, knives, and spears bounced off the creature's foul-smelling hide. But the Beast of Gévaudan—named for the region where she lurked—met her match in early 1765, when she set upon a 12-year-old boy named Jacques Portefaix.

The attacks had begun the year before, when the beast killed a 14-year-old girl. More victims followed. Survivors described a wolf-like creature as large as a donkey—usually female—with reddish fur and a hyena-like black stripe down her back. She moved at supernatural speeds and could swing her tail like a whip. In some accounts, the beast walked upright on her hind legs. Many peasants believed she was a *loup-garou:* French for "werewolf."

In early 1765, the beast set upon a group of seven children tending cattle, snatching the youngest in her jaws. Portefaix, the oldest of the children, led the group in a daring counterattack. Wielding knives and sticks, they chased the beast into a bog until she became stuck in the muck. Portefaix and his pals battled the snarling creature until she finally released her prey and wriggled free to flee into the forest. The victim survived. Portefaix had saved the day! He became a national hero. The king of France was so impressed by the boy's bravery that he rewarded Portefaix with gold and an education.

TO THIS DAY, THE SPECIES OF THE BEAST REMAINS UNKNOWN ...

FEARLESS FACTS

⊃ **BORN:** 1753 ⊃ **DIED:** 1785 ⊃ **OCCUPATION:** Cattle herder ⊃ **BOLDEST MOMENT:** Saving a child from the jaws of a fearsome creature

JOHN HENRY

THE MAN WHO BEAT THE MACHINE

THE STEEL-DRIVING MAN WAS ONE OF AMERICA'S ORIGINAL FOLK HEROES ...

When John Henry went to work, the earth trembled and mountains gave way. As a steel-driver in the 1870s, it was his job to hammer metal rods into rock, smashing holes for explosives that blasted holes for train tunnels. Henry was one of America's original folk heroes, and his was the first tale of man versus machine.

Historians believe the saga of John Henry—sung in songs that lighten the drudgery of hard labor—was based on a real man: a former slave who towered over his fellow steel-drivers in the railroad company. He may have worked on the Big Bend Tunnel through the mountains of West Virginia, U.S.A., or possibly on a tunnel site in Alabama, U.S.A. Regardless of the location, the details of Henry's heroic battle remain the same: Henry up against a steam-powered hammer that supposedly smashed rock faster than any human. Henry took great pride in his work, and he wasn't about to be replaced by a machine.

The day of the race, both man and machine came out swinging. According to legend, Henry—his biceps bulging—hammered away at the mountain for hours and hours. He never tired and never lagged, staying ahead of the machine until it finally, literally, ran out of steam.

Most versions of the tale (and even one supposed eyewitness account) take a tragic turn. With the machine beaten, Henry collapsed to the cave floor and died from exhaustion, still clutching his hammer. Whether the real John Henry keeled over or continued to hammer his way across America, his feat lives on, inspiring us all to move mountains.

FEARLESS FACTS

➔ **BORN:** ca 1840 ➔ **DIED:** 1870s ➔ **OCCUPATION:** Construction worker
➔ **BOLDEST MOMENT:** Beating a steam-powered hammer in a race to build a train tunnel

STRONGER THAN FICTION

Megastrength, superhearing, invulnerability—superpowers are standard issue in comic books and movies, but what about real life? Here are four amazing abilities and the people who wield them ...

FOUR SUPERPOWERED PEOPLE

SUPERSENSES

It's a common belief that people who have a disability—such as blindness or deafness—will develop heightened senses to compensate for that lack of sensory input.

POWER PLAYER: BEN UNDERWOOD

Blinded by cancer at the age of three, California, U.S.A., teenager Ben Underwood taught himself to "see" using echolocation: the technique of bouncing sound off of objects to read their position. (Dolphins and bats use echolocation to see in murky or dark environments.) By making clicking noises with his tongue, Underwood could "see" well enough to play basketball, ride a bicycle, skateboard, and more. Sadly, when he was 16, this inspiring teenager passed away from the same cancer that took his vision.

SUPERSTRENGTH

Superman and Spider-Man can toss sedans like they're paperweights, but even Olympic weightlifters would have a tough time budging the family Buick—unless they're granted so-called hysterical strength: a sudden boost in lifting ability spurred by emergency situations. Although research on hysterical strength is sketchy, some scientists theorize that a sudden shot of adrenaline—a hormone released by your body in moments of crisis—can boost muscles to their maximum potential.

POWER PLAYER: TOM BOYLE, JR.

When a sports car ran over an 18-year-old Arizona bicyclist in 2006, bystander Tom Boyle, Jr., leaped to action, lifting the car off the victim with just his bare hands while the car's driver pulled the man to safety.

SUPERSPEED

No human can outrun a speeding bullet (1,700 miles an hour [2,736 km/h]) or even catch up with the fastest land animal—the cheetah—which achieves speeds of 75 miles an hour (120 km/h). But Olympic sprinters train their entire careers to squeeze every bit of power out of each step.

POWER PLAYER: USAIN BOLT

This aptly named Olympic sprinter is the world's fastest human, reaching average speeds above 23 miles an hour (37 km/h) and top speeds above 27 miles an hour (43 km/h). That might not seem so speedy until you realize it's twice as fast as the average human running speed. Scientists credit Bolt's record-breaking abilities to his height—6 foot, 5 inches (196 cm)—and long legs, which propel him farther and faster while touching the ground fewer times than any other athlete.

INVINCIBILITY

Humans are highly adaptable but hardly indestructible, relying on equipment and ingenuity to survive extreme environments and situations. The average person will overheat—a condition called hyperthermia—after just 10 minutes spent in a humid environment exceeding 140°F (60°C). At the other end of the thermometer, most humans die if their body temperature drops to 70°F (21°C), which can happen if they spend too much time out in the cold or in even slightly chilly water—a condition called hypothermia.

POWER PLAYER: WIM HOF

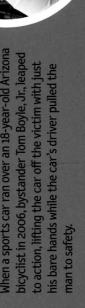

This Dutch daredevil is nicknamed the Iceman for his ability to withstand extreme cold for hours without so much as shivering. He has jogged up some of the world's tallest, iciest mountains wearing nothing but running shorts. He even sat in a bath of ice up to his neck for nearly an hour and 15 minutes to set a Guinness World Record. Hof insists he can override his body's reactions and crank up his internal temperature.

SUPER-HUMANS

CIVITRON

BASE OF OPERATIONS: Salem, Massachusetts, U.S.A.

SUPERPOWER: Amazing marketing skills. Organizes events for charity and street cleanups.

B y day they're accountants and security guards, teachers and gardeners. By night, they don capes and cool costumes before taking to the streets on the lookout for people who need help. They're members of the real-life superhero movement, a worldwide unofficial brother- and sisterhood of average citizens inspired by comic book legends to dress up and try to make the world a better place.

Although they lack superpowers, real-life superheroes share some characteristics with their comic book inspirations. They carry utility belts and backpacks filled with essential neighbor-helping tools: flashlights, cell phones, sturdy cameras, and laser pointers. They have cool superhero names: KnightVigil, The Crimson Fist, and Master Legend, to name a few. Some even have secret identities.

The movement's origin story begins in the late 1990s, when a masked Mexican folk hero calling himself Superbarrio donned red tights and a yellow cape to organize rallies and protests in support of poor families. Today, real-life superheroes take to streets everywhere from Argentina to the United States, handing out food to the homeless, walking people home in dangerous neighborhoods, changing tires, carrying groceries for the elderly, reporting crimes, and engaging in other helpful activities. Some have even formed leagues of like-minded do-gooders, including Team Justice, which takes donations to buy toys for needy children. The Avengers would be proud.

CITIZEN PRIME

BASE OF OPERATIONS Arizona and Utah, U.S.A.

SUPERPOWER: Stellar teaching abilities. His Kid Heroes program inspired schoolchildren to get involved.

SUPERHERO

BASE OF OPERATIONS: Clearwater, Florida, U.S.A.

SUPERPOWER: Astounding powers of sharing. Organizes charity toy drives for underprivileged children.

THANTOS

BASE OF OPERATIONS: Vancouver, British Columbia, Canada

SUPERPOWER: Extreme generosity. Hands out dry socks, rain slickers, and canned food to people living on the streets.

LIFE

BASE OF OPERATIONS: New York, New York, U.S.A.

SUPERPOWER: Outstanding organizational skills. Founded Superheroes Anonymous to unite other real-life superheroes in making a difference.

KING ARTHUR

THE ONCE AND FUTURE KING

He once defended Great Britain and transformed it into a gleaming kingdom. According to legend, he will return to do it again. Tales of King Arthur, a warrior king who rose to power after plucking the sword Excalibur from a stone, have been told in the British Isles since the Middle Ages, gathering twists, quests, and characters in the retelling by different authors. It's a legend rich in magic, romance, and the exploits of gallant knights who met at a round table in Arthur's spectacular castle, Camelot. And like the legend of Robin Hood, King Arthur might have been inspired by a real person. Actually, make that persons.

GOOD KNIGHT

Arthur (or Arturus, as his name is spelled in Latin) is first mentioned by a 9th-century writer as a fearless warlord who defeated tribes of Anglo-Saxon invaders in a series of 12 battles. Arthur supposedly lived at the beginning of the Middle Ages, around the fifth century. His knights would have worn suits of tough leather beneath interwoven iron rings—chainmail armor—rather than the shining plates of steel donned by knights in the 15th century. Arthur, both the man and the myth, inspired a code of good conduct for

FEARLESS FACTS

➔ **BORN:** Some time in the 5th century, Tintagel Castle, England ➔ **DIED:** Some time in the 5th or 6th century, possibly in Queen Camel, England ➔ **OCCUPATION:** Warrior, King of the Britons
➔ **BOLDEST MOMENT:** Defending Britain from Anglo-Saxon invaders

all knights to follow. Chivalrous warriors swore to be generous and humble, protect the old and the weak, treat women with respect, and serve the church.

HOLE IN HISTORY

And yet this chivalrous king isn't mentioned in any major historical accounts written before the 9th century. His absence from history—along with his fanciful feats and magical companions in later tales—led historians to believe Arthur was not a real person. It's more likely he was based on a collection of medieval movers and shakers, inspiring a legend that grew more fantastical through the centuries.

If Arthur's knights met at a round table or quested for the Holy Grail (a gold cup said to grant immortal life), such artifacts have never been found. Poets and writers added elements of romance and magic—including the sword Excalibur—to Arthur's myth beginning in the 12th century. According to *The History of the Kings of Britain*, written around 1138, King Arthur was mortally wounded in his final battle and sailed to the legendary island of Avalon, where he was magically healed of his injuries and got a bonus superpower in the bargain: immortality.

QUEST FOR CAMELOT

At least one part of Arthur's legend, however, may have been uncovered in Somerset, England. It doesn't look like much today, just a grassy hill named Cadbury jutting hundreds of feet above the English countryside. Archaeologists have found evidence that a massive timber castle, protected by four ditches, sat here in the early Middle Ages. Legend has it that a famous warrior king once sat there, in a place called Camelot, and that he will return again when he is most needed.

The Knights of the Round Table assemble (above), and the Holy Grail appears to the knight Percival (right).

DARING DAUGHTER: Hua Mulan (ca A.D. 500)

GUTSY GALS

Disney's 1998 animated movie *Mulan* tells the story of a girl who goes to war so her aging father doesn't have to. But this heroic tale is more than just a story. Like King Arthur, Mulan may have been a real person. She was first mentioned in a 1,500-year-old Chinese poem called "The Ballad of Mulan." In most Chinese families, the sons answered the emperor's call to fight. Mulan had no brothers, so the job fell to her elderly and ailing father. She disguised herself as a man so that she could go in his place. Clutching an ancient sword passed down through her family for generations, Mulan headed off to fight an army of invaders, known as the Huns. She won the respect of her fellow soldiers with her combat skills, which she had learned from her father. Legend says that Mulan fought for 12 years, and each year she was honored by the army with a higher rank. Over time, the name Hua Mulan has come to mean "heroine" in Chinese society.

AWESOME ANCIENTS
HEROES IN MYTHOLOGY

Hercules | SUPERPOWER: Megastrength

Of all the Greek heroes, brawny Hercules has the most interesting origin story. He was the son of a mortal woman and Zeus, the king of the gods. Zeus's goddess wife, Hera, wasn't happy with the situation, and she wasted no time taking it out on her husband's beloved half-god son. She sent poisonous snakes into Hercules' crib, but the muscle-bound baby crushed them before you could say "Goo-goo, ga-gaaahhh!" Hera's harassment of Hercules continued throughout his life. She dreamed up 12 deadly labors for Hercules, such as conquering the three-headed hound Cerberus and a nine-headed serpent called the Hydra. Just like a modern superhero, Hercules always survived for the sequel.

COMIC BOOK EQUIVALENT: The Incredible Hulk

Achilles | SUPERPOWER: Near invincibility

Like Hercules, Achilles had an interesting pair of parents: a king for a dad and a sea spirit named Thetis for a mom. Holding him by an ankle, Thetis dipped baby Achilles into a magical river, making him indestructible from head to toe. He grew up to be a warrior with no equal. A type of fortune teller known as an oracle offered Achilles a prediction of his life's course: He could either pursue glory and die young or live peacefully and die old—and unknown. If he'd chosen the second option, you wouldn't be reading about him. Achilles perished in the Trojan War from an arrow wound to the ankle—the one his mother held above that magic river. Achilles' heel was his only weak spot (which is why the term today describes any weakness).

COMIC BOOK EQUIVALENT: Iron Man

Perseus | *SUPERPOWER:* Cool gadgets

Perseus was another son of Zeus and a mortal mother. He lacked the brawn of his half brother Hercules, but he made up for it with quick thinking. He also wielded cool magic gadgets, including winged sandals, a helmet of invisibility, and a shield with a built-in mirror. The mirror came in handy when Perseus set out to slay Medusa—a part-female, part-monster creature with snakes in place of hair—whose gaze had the power to turn men into stone. He used the shield's reflection to avoid Medusa's scary stare. Once Medusa was dead, Perseus had another bright idea: He used her head as a weapon to petrify the Kraken, a fearsome sea creature poised to devour the princess Andromeda.

COMIC BOOK EQUIVALENT: Batman

Odysseus | *SUPERPOWER:* Supersmarts

This clever Greek king hatched the greatest ruse in the history of warfare: the Trojan Horse. The citizens of Troy mistook this titanic wooden horse as a parting gift from the Greeks after a long siege. They opened their city gates, hauled in the horse, and partied late into the night. As the Trojans slept off their celebration, Greek soldiers hidden in the horse's belly emerged and reopened the city gates for the Greek army. Odysseus' victory over the Trojans is but one chapter in an odyssey that has him outsmarting a who's who of mythological monsters, from the Cyclops to the shipwrecking Sirens.

COMIC BOOK EQUIVALENT:
Mr. Fantastic

Atalanta

SUPERPOWER: Athletic skill

Faster than any Olympic sprinter, deadlier with a bow than Hawkeye from the Avengers, Atalanta was the ultimate athlete. Men could not resist her beauty or grace, but she vowed never to marry anyone who couldn't beat her in a race. She was the only female crew member of the *Argo,* the ship of legendary heroes who quested for the Golden Fleece. Afterward, she used her super-human hunting abilities to slay a monstrous boar that was terrorizing the countryside.

COMIC BOOK EQUIVALENT: Wonder Woman

LUKE SKYWALKER

THE FORCE WILL BE WITH HIM, ALWAYS

Brsssh! Vrrmm! Bisssh! Hrrmm! Even if you've never made lightsaber noises while swinging a flashlight, you probably know a little about Luke Skywalker: the Jedi knight, the ace starfighter pilot, the good guy with the bad dad. The central character of the original *Star Wars* trilogy, he's a hero everyone can root for. There's a reason he's so relatable: Luke's story really is from a long time ago, if not exactly a galaxy far, far away.

George Lucas, original mastermind of the *Star Wars* universe, followed a formula called the hero's journey when he plotted the course of his movies. It's a set of events identified by American scholar Joseph Campbell after he researched thousands of years of storytelling, going back to the earliest tales told around flickering campfires. Ancient legends and religious tales might not have X-Wing starfighters or Wookiee sidekicks, but they all share similar elements: a hero yearning for adventure, help from the supernatural, a series of trials, occasional conflicts with a father figure, and ultimately a victory over impossible odds and freedom from evil.

Sound familiar? Our hero Luke leaves his desert planet and learns to wield a mystical Force to rescue his friends. Along the way, he loses his Jedi mentor before settling his differences with Darth Vader, a sinister man in black who (spoiler alert!) is also his old man. Eventually, Luke saves the galaxy from an evil empire. His adventures have been a part of pop culture for decades; Luke's journey has been part of culture for much longer.

> "... I WARN YOU NOT TO UNDERESTIMATE MY POWERS."
> —LUKE SKYWALKER

FEARLESS FACTS

→ **BORN:** A long time ago, in a galaxy far, far away → **OCCUPATION:** Jedi knight
→ **BOLDEST MOMENT:** Making a one-in-a-million shot to blow up the planet-smashing Death Star

HARRY POTTER

A MODERN MYTH FOR MUGGLES

Saying Harry Potter is popular is a pretty epic understatement: Author Joanne "J. K." Rowling's creation has become a fixture of modern mythology, spawning blockbuster movies, an endless line of toys, and even a theme park. No doubt you know the basics of the Boy Who Lived, so nicknamed after his parents gave their lives protecting an infant Harry Potter from the evil Lord Voldemort (aka He-Who-Must-Not-Be-Named). Over the course of seven best-selling novels, the orphaned Harry Potter is whisked from the world of muggles (non-magical folks), learns the ways of witchcraft and wizardry, thwarts countless attempts on his life by Voldemort and his allies, and discovers the one thing more powerful than magic is friendship.

Potter's journey from hard-luck orphan to hero of the wizard world mirrors Rowling's own rise above difficult situations. The author began writing her enchanted tale during a trying time. Rowling's mother was dying of an illness, which inspired her story of an orphan's battle with evil. Low on money and raising her daughter alone, she saw her story rejected 12 times in the mid-1990s. Finally, an editor at a publishing company showed the first chapter of her manuscript to his eight-year-old daughter, who couldn't wait to read what happened next. *Harry Potter and the Philosopher's Stone* (known as *Harry Potter and the Sorcerer's Stone* in the U.S.) was published in 1997. The book became a smash with legions of readers who couldn't wait to see what happened next. Today, Rowling is one of the world's most famous muggles, as inspiring as her spellbinding hero.

"WORKING HARD IS IMPORTANT. BUT THERE IS SOMETHING THAT MATTERS EVEN MORE, BELIEVING IN YOURSELF."
—HARRY POTTER

FEARLESS FACTS

→ **BORN:** July 31, 1980, Godric's Hollow, England → **OCCUPATION:** Student at Hogwarts School of Witchcraft and Wizardry → **BOLDEST MOMENT:** Facing certain death in a confrontation with the villainous Lord Voldemort

MOMENT OF BRAVERY

This unlikely hero felt compelled to act. How did Tank Man make history?

THE SCENARIO

An iron suit might seem like a more suitable ensemble for any hero with the power to stop a 40-ton (36-t) tank, but the Chinese pedestrian known only as Tank Man wore black slacks and a white shirt while wielding a bag of groceries in each hand. Just past noon on June 5, 1989, this daring soul was walking along a street in Beijing, China, when he felt a tremor beneath his feet. A column of tanks was rumbling down the road in his direction! The tanks were closing in on Tiananmen Square, where just the day before the Chinese military had attacked hundreds of students protesting government corruption. What happened next turned Tank Man into a legend. He stepped off the sidewalk and into the history books.

THE MOMENT OF TRUTH

Perhaps he wanted to stand up for the students in Tiananmen Square, or maybe he thought one man could make a difference against these war machines. No one knows what Tank Man was thinking when he walked calmly in front of the column of tanks. The lead machine was mere feet from hitting the man when its driver put on the brakes, bringing the column to a halt. Onlookers gasped. Journalists aimed their cameras. They thought they were watching Tank Man make his last stand, a repeat of the previous day's violence.

Tank Man refused to step aside in the face of certain death. When the lead tank tried to skirt around him, he stepped in front of it, stopping it again and again. Finally, Tank Man climbed atop the tank and exchanged a few words with its driver, who displayed his own special courage by refusing to run down a defenseless man. Their conversation remains a mystery to this day. The entire exchange lasted just two minutes before concerned onlookers rushed Tank Man off the road. His identity remains unknown.

THE LEGACY

The scene was captured on video and is one of the 20th century's most iconic photos of bravery. But courage was on display on the other side of the lens, as well. The Chinese government didn't allow journalists to take photos or video without official approval; footage and film had to be sneaked out of the country. Photographers caught breaking the rules could be thrown in jail. The most widely seen picture of Tank Man was smuggled out in a box of tea.

Images of Tank Man's brave stand made the front pages of newspapers and magazines across the world, going viral in the days before the Internet. The scene spoke for itself in any language: one man against impossible might. The photos were a public-relations disaster for the Chinese government, which faced worldwide ridicule and costly economic penalties for its treatment of the protesters. Tank Man had shown the world that one courageous act can make a difference.

CHAPTER THREE

GAME CHANGERS

Most professional athletes get paid a fortune to work just half the year doing a job they love. We idolize them, ask them for autographs, and throw them parades. But this chapter isn't about those kinds of good sports. Instead, get ready to give a hero's welcome to the champions who championed a cause, the competitors who rose to the top against all odds, and the athletes who changed the world as well as the world of sports. These game changers went above and beyond the field to inspire everyone, not just their fans.

Stunt rider Robbie "Maddo" Maddison surfs through the waves of Tahiti on a motorbike.

49

JESSE OWENS

AMERICA'S FIRST OLYMPIC HERO

"ONE CHANCE IS ALL YOU NEED."
–JESSE OWENS

The eyes of the world were on Jesse Owens at the 1936 Olympic Games in Berlin, Germany, and not just because he was a record-setting athlete with a winning personality. Held in Germany under Adolf Hitler's Nazi regime, these summer games were about more than the thrill of international competition. The Nazi Party believed in a poisonous myth: that Jewish and black people were inferior. These games were the Nazis' opportunity to showcase the supposed superiority of Germany's Aryan "race." Hitler was certain his nation's athletes would dominate every event. Jesse Owens, the black grandson of slaves, was poised to prove him wrong.

FEARLESS FACTS

➲ **BORN:** September 12, 1913, Oakville, Alabama, U.S.A. ➲ **DIED:** March 31, 1980, Tucson, Arizona, U.S.A.
➲ **OCCUPATION:** Track-and-field athlete, speaker ➲ **BOLDEST MOMENT:** Winning four gold medals at the 1936 Olympics and humiliating the Nazi Party

BERLIN BOUND

James Cleveland Owens (nicknamed Jesse by a teacher who misunderstood Owens's pronunciation of "J. C.") always took the lead. As a boy in Alabama, U.S.A., he sprinted through the fields where he helped his family pick cotton. As a teenager, he raced through the streets of Cleveland, Ohio, U.S.A., and became a renowned track star at his high school. He achieved one of the greatest feats in sports history in 1935 as a sophomore at Ohio State University. Owens broke five world records and tied for a sixth, all in less than an hour, at a track-and-field championship—while he was suffering from a back injury! As a junior, he competed in 42 events and won them all. Owens was a shoo-in for the United States' Olympic track team in Berlin the following year.

He was joined on the team by nine other black athletes—all of them considered inferior by the Nazis. With Hitler watching from the stands, Owens took his mark for the 100-meter (328-foot) dash. *Bang!* The race was on! Just 10.3 seconds later, Owens practically flew across the finish line as the winner. Over the next week in Berlin, he set three world records and won three more gold medals—a first for a track-and-field star at a single Olympics. His sportsmanship won over the German spectators in the stadium. They chanted his name even as Hitler ignored him. For the Nazis, Owens's triumph was a defeat.

A HERO'S UNWELCOME

Owens received a parade and accolades when he returned to the United States, but not everyone gave him the star treatment. Owens was turned away from hotels and restaurants because of the color of his skin. And the president of the United States never called to congratulate Owens or invite him to the White House.

But Owens succeeded despite these setbacks. He became a popular speaker and traveled the world as a Goodwill Ambassador for the United States. In 1976, President Gerald Ford presented Owens with the Presidential Medal of Freedom. The recognition was long overdue.

Owens on the podium after winning gold in Berlin (above) and on a commemorative stamp issued in 1990 (right)

SUPERWOMAN: Jackie Joyner-Kersee (1962–)

GUTSY GALS

Sports Illustrated magazine once put her photo on the cover next to the words "Super Woman," a title she more than lived up to: Olympic champion Jackie Joyner-Kersee holds three golds, a silver, and two bronzes—the most medals of any woman in Olympic track-and-field history. Her event was the heptathlon, a grueling challenge that combines seven sports in one: a 100-meter (328-foot) hurdle race, the high jump, shot put, a 200-meter (656-foot) race, the long jump, the javelin throw, and, finally, an 800-meter (2,625-foot) race. The heptathlon tests speed, flexibility, precision, and raw strength, and it's one of the toughest events in the Olympic Games. Joyner-Kersee still holds the world record for heptathlon today—and the next five highest scores, too.

GOOD SPORTS
FEARLESS OFF THE FIELD

Everyone cheered when these ultimate team players took the field or the court, but their most inspiring moves continued beyond the sidelines and after the final buzzer. Meet five champions who answered a higher calling outside the world of sports.

BATTER UPWARD: Ted Williams (1918–2002)

Ted Williams didn't play baseball to impress the press or make friends with fans in the stands. He played to hit the ball. Williams literally wrote the book on batting (called *The Science of Hitting*, written in 1970 and still studied by players today), and he's often named the greatest hitter in major league history. His hit count would've been higher if he hadn't traded the baseball bat for the flight stick, becoming a Navy flight instructor in World War II. He returned to the cockpit to fly 39 combat missions during the Korean War. Although his military service kept him from the baseball diamond during his prime years, Williams never complained or expressed regrets. When he retired from the Boston Red Sox, in 1960, Teddy Ballgame gave the fans what they wanted: His final hit was a home run.

KING OF THE COURT: Arthur Ashe (1943–1993)

When he picked up a tennis racket for the first time, in 1950, seven-year-old Arthur Ashe wasn't allowed to play in the segregated (or whites-only) indoor tennis courts of Richmond, Virginia, U.S.A. Eighteen years later, he became the first black player to win the U.S. Open. He won the Wimbledon singles' championship—the oldest and most coveted title in tennis—in 1975. Against all odds, he had conquered the tennis world and championed the cause of black athletes, but his greatest battles were still ahead. In 1983, he was infected with the HIV virus from a blood transfusion. Until his death from AIDS-related pneumonia, in 1993, Ashe made it his mission to spread awareness of HIV and AIDS and help fund its cure. In 1993, sports network ESPN created the annual Arthur Ashe Courage Award—an award earned by several of the heroes in this chapter.

GRIDIRON WARRIOR: Pat Tillman (1976–2004)

Pat Tillman was not a typical jock. While attending Arizona State University on a football scholarship in 1997, he was a winner on the field (helping his team through an undefeated season) and in the classroom (winning numerous academic awards). The following year, he'd achieved the dream of every young football player: He'd become a pro in the National Football League, picked as a linebacker for the Arizona Cardinals.

But after the attacks of September 11, 2001, Tillman decided that sports were not as important as serving his country. Putting his football dreams on hold, he joined the U.S. Army, even though it meant turning down a three-year, multimillion-dollar contract with the Cardinals and leaving behind a life of luxury and celebrity. Tillman became an Army Ranger, part of an elite force, and served tours of duty in the world's most dangerous regions. Then, in 2004, he was accidentally killed by friendly fire while trying to rescue his comrades from an ambush. To honor Tillman's pursuit of excellence and his sense of duty, his family established the Pat Tillman Foundation, which grants college scholarships to military veterans and their spouses who share Tillman's talents for leadership and public service.

THE UNBREAKABLE MAN: Louis Zamperini (1917–2014)

Like his American track-and-field teammate Jesse Owens, Louis "Louie" Zamperini competed in front of Adolf Hitler at the 1936 Summer Olympics in Berlin. Seven years later, Zamperini was fighting against Hitler and Germany's Japanese allies as a bomber crewman in World War II. His Olympic endurance was put to the ultimate test in 1943, when his plane crashed in the Pacific. The military assumed he was dead; his parents even received a condolence letter from the U.S. president. But Zamperini was adrift in a life raft. After 43 days battling sharks and eating raw fish, he was captured by the Japanese Navy and spent the next two years enduring torture and other horrors in prisoner-of-war camps. His captors beat his body, but Zamperini's spirit remained unbroken. He returned home to a hero's welcome in 1945. He later forgave his Japanese guards and used his hardships to encourage others never to give up. At the 1998 Winter Olympics in Nagano, Japan, 80-year-old Zamperini ran a leg with the Olympic Torch not far from the camp where he had been held captive.

THREE-POINT PATRIOT: Manute Bol (1962–2010)

At seven feet six inches (2.3 m) tall, Manute Bol may or may not have been the most towering player in the history of professional basketball (he tied for height with another basketball star). Without a doubt, though, he was the player with the biggest heart. Born in war-ravaged South Sudan, Africa, Bol donated much of the salary he earned during his ten-year career as one of the NBA's top shot blockers to helping refugees in his home country and to causes that promote peace. He once even signed a one-day contract with a hockey team—despite his clumsiness on ice skates—to raise money for his countrymen. It's no wonder Bol's friend and fellow basketball star Charles Barkley said, "If everyone in the world was a Manute Bol, it's a world I'd want to live in."

MUHAMMAD ALI

THE PEOPLE'S CHAMPION

Muhammad Ali called himself "the greatest." Few disagreed. He won a gold medal in boxing at the 1960 Olympics and became the world heavyweight champion four years later. Out of 61 fights, he lost only five. But not all of Ali's battles were in the ring.

Born Cassius Marcellus Clay, Jr., in 1942, the future champ grew up in the American South, where black people weren't allowed to use the same public places, schools, restaurants, and drinking fountains as white people. These "Jim Crow laws" left an impression on the young man. When the fuming 12-year-old Clay wanted to pummel a thief who stole his bike, a police officer saw a chance to channel the boy's anger into something constructive: He taught Clay how to box.

Clay's wit was as fast as his footwork. Crowds loved how he taunted opponents during matches. Outside of boxing, he was just as fearless and outspoken, especially on the matter of civil rights for black people. In 1964, he joined the Nation of Islam, a black Muslim group, and changed his name to Muhammad Ali. Not long after, he was arrested for refusing to fight in the Vietnam War for religious reasons. Ali knew that his convictions would cost him. Banned from boxing and stripped of his titles, he traveled the country speaking against the war and for civil rights causes.

After the U.S. Supreme Court supported his religious objections, Ali returned to the ring in 1970 and regained the heavyweight title. He retired in 1981 and has spent much of his time since working for charities. He remains one of the world's most well-respected athletes—a man who never backed down.

> "IF MY MIND CAN CONCEIVE IT, AND MY HEART CAN BELIEVE IT—THEN I CAN ACHIEVE IT."
> —MUHAMMAD ALI

FEARLESS FACTS

➔ **BORN:** January 17, 1942, Louisville, Kentucky, U.S.A. ➔ **OCCUPATION:** Professional boxer
➔ **BOLDEST MOMENT:** Risking his boxing career by refusing to fight in the Vietnam War because of his religious beliefs

MICHAEL JORDAN

HIS ROYAL AIRNESS

He led the Chicago Bulls to win six championships and took home eight Most Valuable Player awards (not to mention two Olympic gold medals), but Michael Jordan—aka MJ—is considered the world's greatest basketball player for more than just his stats. Jordan turned every throw into an air show. He soared toward the basket, defying the laws of physics, seeming to change direction in midair. Jordan's opponents on the court envied his skills. Fans idolized him. Everyone wanted to be "like Mike," paying hundreds of dollars to wear a pair of his Air Jordan shoes.

After leading the Chicago Bulls to a "three-peat"—winning three consecutive championships—Jordan shocked the sports world in 1993 by stepping off the basketball court and onto the baseball field. Jordan had been devastated by the recent death of his father, who had dreamed that Jordan would become a Major League Baseball player. Jordan signed a contract with the Chicago White Sox to play on its minor league farm teams. His batting, running, and fielding skills were not up to snuff for even minor league ball, although fans and teammates treated him with a mix of respect and curiosity. But Jordan's abysmal season in baseball renewed his passion for basketball. In 1995, Air Jordan soared again. He returned to the Chicago Bulls and helped the team achieve another three-peat before retiring, in 1999.

> "I CAN ACCEPT FAILURE, EVERYONE FAILS AT SOMETHING. BUT I CAN'T ACCEPT NOT TRYING."
> —MICHAEL JORDAN

FEARLESS FACTS

→ **BORN:** February 17, 1963, Brooklyn, New York, U.S.A. → **OCCUPATION:** Professional basketball player
→ **BOLDEST MOMENT:** Making The Shot: his famous buzzer-beating, series-winning basket against the Cleveland Cavaliers in 1989

FIGHTING WORDS
BOLDEST SPEECHES IN SPORTS

Along with Gatorade showers and the seventh-inning stretch, inspiring speeches are a timeless sports tradition. They're equal parts pep talk and theater, meant to transform disheartened teams of losers into unstoppable winners. But the most encouraging words rose above the arena.

Vince Lombardi, *FOOTBALL COACH* (1913–1970)

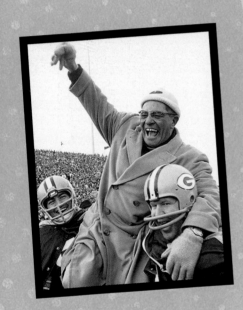

As a football player at New York's Fordham University, Vince Lombardi was one of the Seven Blocks of Granite: the team's invincible offensive line. But he learned he could lead men as well as bash them when he became head coach for the Green Bay Packers in 1959. At the time, the Packers were the worst team in the National Football League. By his second season, Lombardi had coached them to the Western Conference title. He led them to win the very first Super Bowl championship, in 1967. When the Packers returned for Super Bowl II against the Oakland Raiders a year later, Lombardi delivered a legendary pregame pep talk ...

What he said: "[The Raiders are] going to try to hit you, and you got to take it most of the time. You got to be 40 tigers out there. That's all. Just hit. Just run. Just block and just tackle. If you do that, there's no question what the answer's going to be in this ballgame. Keep your poise. You've faced them all. There's nothing they can show you out there you haven't faced a number of times."

After the words: The Packers beat the Raiders to win Super Bowl II. Lombardi became a six-time NFL champion and went down in history as one of its greatest coaches.

Herb Brooks, *OLYMPIC HOCKEY COACH* (1937–2003)

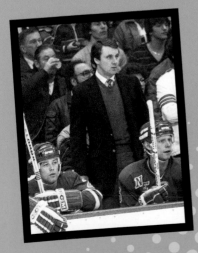

It was the hockey equivalent of David versus Goliath: 20 amateur hockey players, mostly teenagers, versus a veteran team tested in years of international competition. The U.S. national hockey team was facing off against the Soviet Union's pro-level players at the 1980 Winter Olympics at Lake Placid, New York. Relations between the two countries had reached a deep freeze after decades of Cold War superpower rivalry, but American coach Herb Brooks kept a cool head. His players may have been the underdogs, but Brooks drilled confidence into them. His pregame speech, jotted on an envelope, was immortalized in the 2004 movie *Miracle*.

What he said: "You were born to be hockey players. You were meant to be here at this moment. You were meant to be here at this game ... I'm sick and tired of hearing about what a great hockey team the Soviets have ... This is your time. Now go out there and take it!"

Jim Valvano,
COLLEGE BASKETBALL COACH (1946–1993)

After leading his North Carolina State Wolfpack to victory in the 1983 college basketball championships—against a team that had been undefeated for 26 games—coach Jim Valvano famously jogged up and down the court looking for someone to hug. Ten years later, there wasn't a sports fan in America who didn't want to hug Valvano back. ESPN had awarded this coach, better known as Jimmy V, the network's first courage award for his motivational speeches and fearlessness in the face of a deadly disease: He had been diagnosed with a painful form of cancer a year before. You would never know it when he took the podium for his acceptance speech.

What he said: "To me, there are three things we all should do every day ... Number one is laugh ... Number two is think ... Number three is you should have your emotions moved to tears, could be happiness or joy ... If you laugh, you think and you cry, that's a full day ... You do that seven days a week, you're going to have something special ... Cancer can take away all of my physical abilities. It cannot touch my mind, it cannot touch my heart, and it cannot touch my soul. And those three things are going to carry on forever."

After the words: Jimmy V died of his disease less than two months after his famous speech, but his message lives on, along with the V Foundation for Cancer Research. Its motto: "Don't give up ... Don't ever give up!"

Lou Gehrig, MAJOR LEAGUE
BASEBALL PLAYER (1903–1941)

Nothing—not even horrible back pain—could keep Lou Gehrig off the field. He was the New York Yankee's Iron Horse, playing 2,130 consecutive games though the 1920s and 1930s (a streak that held until 1995). But in 1938, Gehrig's skills began slipping. Home runs became pop flies. Base runs were more like jogs. He stumbled in the outfield. It took the diagnosis of a serious illness— a progressive neurodegenerative disease called ALS—to end Gehrig's streak of consecutive games. On May 2, 1939, choking back tears, he took to the field at Yankee Stadium for one last time to deliver his farewell speech to more than 62,000 fans.

What he said: "Fans, for the past two weeks you have been reading about the bad break I got. Yet today I consider myself the luckiest man on the face of this earth. I have been in ballparks for seventeen years and have never received anything but kindness and encouragement from you fans ... When everybody down to the groundskeepers and those boys in white coats remember you with trophies—that's something ... When you have a father and a mother who work all their lives so you can have an education and build your body—it's a blessing. When you have a wife who has been a tower of strength and shown more courage than you dreamed existed—that's the finest I know. So I close in saying that I might have been given a bad break, but I've got an awful lot to live for."

After the words: Gehrig was inducted into the Baseball Hall of Fame. He began working with troubled young people in his retirement, but his disease took its toll on his health. He died in 1941.

After the words: With 20 seconds left on the clock and the American team winning by one point, the home-country crowd began counting down. Ten seconds left. Five. The crowd was on its feet. Three, two ... The buzzer sounded and the crowd erupted into cheers. Americans watching the game on TV heard sportscaster Al Michaels shout the words that defined this moment in sports history. "Do you believe in miracles? YES!" The American underdogs had beaten the Soviet juggernaut 4 to 3 and went on to take the gold medal. *Sports Illustrated* magazine later named the Miracle on Ice the top sports moment of the 20th century.

RAMP CHAMP

SKATE GREAT TONY HAWK TALKS ABOUT HIS UPS AND DOWNS

S kateboarding had a bad rep as a brash pastime until a skinny kid from California, U.S.A., took the sport to new height—literally. Tony Hawk got his first skateboard from his big brother at the age of nine. Seven years later, he was one of the sport's top stars, specializing in high-flying tricks launched off of U-shaped half-pipe ramps. Soaring higher than other competitors (hence his nickname: the Birdman), Hawk made history in 1999 as the first skater to spin 900 degrees—or two and a half turns—and land without falling. Now, anyone can fly like the Birdman in Activision's popular Tony Hawk's Pro Skater series of video games, which propelled skateboarding into the mainstream. In 2009, Hawk became the first pro skateboarder to ride at the White House. His brash pastime had become respectable. Meet the Chairman of the Board who made it happen.

Q: Do you think you would still have gotten into skateboarding if your brother hadn't given you your first skateboard?

A: Skating was something that was around me anyway, and a lot of my friends were doing it, but perhaps I wouldn't have tried it. I never really thought of myself as that physically gifted. I wasn't awkward or anything, but when I tried other sports—basketball and baseball and whatnot—I didn't excel at them. Even when I tried skating, I wasn't better than anyone else. But once I discovered what was possible with it, and what people were doing with skateboards in terms of literally flying out of empty swimming pools, that's when it clicked for me. That's when I knew it was something I wanted to pursue. I wanted to learn how to do those maneuvers.

Q: Before skateboarding became second nature, how did you build up courage to drop down that ramp?

A: I started small and worked my way up to it. It was more about having the confidence. All along I was telling myself I was capable of things, even though I wasn't sure of it. That really set me apart from a lot of my friends, but it also allowed me to keep trying things that nobody had tried before ... If you visualize yourself doing the things that you dream of, you can make them reality. A lot of my friends would visualize their worst-case scenarios instead. If you think in those terms, that's what comes to reality.

Q: But you had your share of "worst-case scenarios," too. How did you push past your injuries?

A: Early on, when I first learned how to get to the top of a pool—you'd do what's called a rock-and-roll, which is where you rock your board at the top of the pool and lean in—I got caught up and fell straight on my face. I got a concussion and knocked my teeth out. But when I woke up from that injury, my first thought was, "I want to go back and learn to do it right." That was my moment of truth. I was sitting there feeling my front teeth missing and thinking how could I go back and learn that trick properly.

Q: Describe in one word what it felt like when you landed the 900 in 1999?

A: "Finally!" It was something I had tried so many times in my life that I thought it might not be possible. I just couldn't believe it finally worked. It all happened so fast. In that moment, it was more of a shock.

Q: You were described as hyperactive when you were a child. What advice do you have for kids with similar personalities?

A: Just try a lot of different activities until you find one that suits your personality. And when you find something that is really fulfilling, learn everything about it—the literature about it, history of it, and different techniques about it. Don't just focus on one aspect of what you love doing. In the end you're going to have an advantage over the next person who's interested in it.

Q: Your parents were encouraging of your skateboarding as a kid. How important was their support in your overall success?

A: It helped greatly, because most of my friends' parents didn't want them skating. And so my parents were the ones that gave rides to the other kids to the skate parks. What I was doing was considered unorthodox and something that didn't necessarily have a future, but my parents already had three children and I came late, so they had done everything already. They were supportive of my different interests.

Q: When you were a kid skating around San Diego, did you ever think you'd be invited to ride at the White House grounds one day?

A: No, of course not. I still can't believe that. In fact I got an invite to their holiday party. It's still baffling to me. I'm not sure if they're going to let me bring my skateboard again.

59

JACKIE ROBINSON

THE MAN WHO BROKE BASEBALL'S COLOR BARRIER

"THERE'S NOT AN AMERICAN IN THIS COUNTRY FREE UNTIL EVERY ONE OF US IS FREE."
-JACKIE ROBINSON

Batting averages, fielding percentages, runs, hits, errors—baseball is a numbers game for fans who memorize the statistics of their favorite players. But one number is celebrated above the rest: 42, the jersey number of baseball's most inspiring pioneer, Jack Roosevelt "Jackie" Robinson. He signed with the Brooklyn Dodgers in 1947, back when black and white players competed in separate—or segregated—leagues. When Robinson took the field for the Dodgers, the American civil rights movement had barely begun. Robinson gave it its first home run.

LOADED BASES

On the baseball diamond, Jackie Robinson was powerful at bat and fast in the field, with a talent for stealing bases. He was named the most valuable player of his amateur league long before he earned the same title in the major leagues. But when the United States entered World War II, his sports career was put on hold. In 1942, he was drafted into the U.S. Army.

As in baseball, southern schools, and other aspects of American life at the time, the military was segregated. When Robinson took a stand against segregation in the Army by refusing to move to the back of a military bus, he

FEARLESS FACTS

➔ **BORN:** January 31, 1919, Cairo, Georgia, U.S.A. ➔ **DIED:** October 24, 1972, Stamford, Connecticut, U.S.A.
➔ **OCCUPATION:** Major League Baseball player ➔ **BOLDEST MOMENT:** Enduring threats and racial slurs after taking the field as the first black player in the major leagues

was arrested and court-martialed. Robinson fought the charges and won his acquittal, in part because of his stellar service record. When he left the Army in 1944, Robinson returned to baseball. He began his career as a pro player in the black baseball league.

PLAYING IT COOL

Back on the baseball diamond, Robinson's batting and fielding skills caught the attention of Branch Rickey, president and general manager of the all-white Brooklyn Dodgers. Rickey wanted to bring black players into the major leagues, and he believed Robinson was the guy for the job. Both men knew that breaking baseball's color barrier wouldn't be easy. On April 15, 1947, at the age of 28, Robinson played his first game at Brooklyn's Ebbets Field for the Dodgers' season opener.

He faced hostility from the start. Spectators and opposing players jeered. Pitchers tried to bean (hit) Robinson with the ball at home plate. Off the field, he received hate mail and death threats. But through all the taunting and adversity, Robinson kept his cool and held his head high—a form of peaceful protest that inspired the tactics of the civil rights movement to come. Robinson fought back by playing better than anybody. He was named Rookie of the Year in 1947 and, two years later, won the National League's Most Valuable Player Award. In 1955, Robinson helped the Dodgers win the World Series.

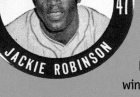

MAGIC NUMBER

Robinson's sportsmanship and skill won over the skeptics. He became a hero to black and white athletes alike and a champion for civil rights within and outside sports. In 1997, Major League Baseball retired Robinson's jersey number throughout the entire league. You'll never see 42 on the field except on Jackie Robinson Day, each April 15, when every player wears that number to celebrate the day baseball's greatest hero made history.

Robinson slides into home during the 1955 World Series.

TEAM PLAYERS: GUYS ON ROBINSON'S SIDE

⮕ EDDIE STANKY (bottom left): Robinson promised to keep calm on the field when he was taunted by opposing players. Teammate Eddie Stanky never made such a promise. He rose to Robinson's defense, shouting down the haters and inspiring teammates to do the same.

⮕ HAROLD PETER HENRY "PEE WEE" REESE (bottom center): This Dodgers shortstop put his arm around Robinson during a game, silencing spectators jeering from the stands. "You can hate a man for many reasons," Reese said. "Color is not one of them."

⮕ LEO DUROCHER (bottom right): When some of Robinson's own teammates threatened to sit out rather than play with a black player, manager Durocher said he would sooner trade them than Robinson.

GOING TO EXTREMES
ACTION SPORTS STARS

Look, up in the sky! It's a bird! It's a plane! It's a bunch of gutsy guys defying gravity—and death! Thrill to the skills (and spills) of daredevil athletes who set aside fear and grabbed their gear to go higher, faster, and/or farther than their competitors in some of the world's most dangerous sports.

WILD RIDER: Robbie Maddison
(1981–)

This Australian motocross star makes the impossible look ... well, still impossible. Maddison (aka Maddo) doesn't just leap landmarks—from Greek canals to football stadiums—he often performs outrageous tricks in the process: He even did a backflip while leaping over the opened Tower Bridge, in London, England! Riding a motorcycle equipped with skis, Maddo—who's held world records for longest distance jumped on a motorcycle—even managed to surf a dangerous monster wave in Tahiti. Some consider him a modern-day Evel Knievel, the legendary landmark-leaping daredevil of the 1970s.

FALLING STAR: Felix Baumgartner
(1969–)

Sixty-five years after test pilot Chuck Yeager broke the sound barrier in a roaring jet airplane, this Austrian professional skydiver flew faster than the speed of sound—reaching nearly 850 miles an hour (1,368 km/h)—using nothing but the force of gravity. In October 2012, Baumgartner rode a helium balloon to the edge of space, 24 miles (39 km) above Roswell, New Mexico, U.S.A. He saluted his capsule's cameras, then stepped into the void, plummeting to Earth in a space suit. Baumgartner nearly spun out of control before deploying his parachute, landing safely on the ground ten minutes after beginning his one giant leap. He had set the record for the highest skydiving jump.

MOUNTAIN MEN: Tommy Caldwell and Kevin Jorgeson (1978–) and (1984–)

After nearly three weeks of hanging from a sheer mountainside, their fingertips bandaged and bleeding, this dynamic climbing duo reached the summit of El Capitan in California's Yosemite National Park in 2015. They weren't the first men to scramble up the Dawn Wall—considered one of the climbing world's most treacherous routes—but they were the first to free-climb it: using only their fingertips and feet to wedge into crevices and grip narrow ledges like Spider-Man without his sticky superpowers. (Free climbers still wear harnesses and ropes as a safety precaution.) The duo had practiced together for five years and failed in previous attempts, but they always stuck together through good climbs and bad. When Jorgeson got stymied by a tricky stretch of wall for ten days, Caldwell waited and offered encouragement from their dangling tent (called a portaledge), risking his own summiting success. Eventually, teamwork took them to the top.

ACE OF BASE: Lonnie Bissonnette (1965–)

This Canadian athlete knew something had gone wrong when he leaped off a 486-foot (148-m)-tall bridge in 1984 and felt his parachute tangle around his ankle. Bissonnette crashed into the river below at 70 miles an hour (113 km/h), breaking his neck and injuring his spinal cord. His doctor said he would never walk again or participate in his favorite sport: BASE jumping (BASE stands for Buildings, Antennas, Spans, and Earth—the types of fixed features from which these daredevil parachutists plummet). Bissonnette was determined to prove his doctor at least half wrong. Less than a year after his accident, he was back to BASE jumping in a wheelchair modified with its own parachute. He became the first partially paralyzed skydiver to leap from all four BASE objects, including that bridge where he had his brush with death.

DOWNHILL RACER: GUTSY GALS Lindsey Vonn (1984–)

The only American woman ever to win a gold medal for downhill skiing, Lindsey Vonn is considered by many to be the top female skier in the world. She has flown downhill at speeds exceeding 84 miles an hour (135 km/h)—faster than you are legally allowed to drive down most highways! It's her determination that makes her a champion: She spends as many as seven hours in the gym every day, six days a week. In 2013, after experiencing some heavy crashes on the slopes that necessitated knee surgery and months of rehabilitation, Vonn vowed to come back better than ever. And in 2015, with her 63rd victory, Vonn became the winningest woman in World Cup history.

TERRY FOX

THE MAN WHO RAN FOR YOUR LIFE

"I WANT TO SHOW THAT JUST BECAUSE [PEOPLE] ARE DISABLED, IT'S NOT THE END."
–TERRY FOX

Drenching downpours, scorching highways, and frigid gales couldn't stop Terry Fox, a Canadian college student who attempted to run across Canada in the spring in 1980. Fox was determined to finish his intended 5,000-mile (8,047-km) trek despite long stretches of remote roads, rotten weather, and one other obstacle that he considered a source of strength instead of a handicap: his artificial leg.

Fox had been an 18-year-old athlete when he was diagnosed with bone cancer. During his 16 months of treatment—which included his leg being amputated above the knee—he watched fellow cancer patients suffer and die from the illness. He was determined to help.

Fox planned a one-man Marathon of Hope: a cross-country jog to raise cancer awareness and money to fund a cure. He jogged the equivalent of a marathon (26 miles [42 km]) every day along remote roads and jammed city streets. His effort attracted little attention and few donations at first, but soon enthusiasm—and donations—began to grow. Then, two-thirds of the way through his cross-country journey, Fox started feeling out of breath. His cancer had returned and spread to his lungs. Cancer claimed his life in June 1981, when he was just 22 years old.

In total, Fox had managed to cover 3,339 miles (5,374 km) through six Canadian provinces. Despite ending early, Fox's Marathon of Hope has an enduring legacy: It is now an annual event that has raised more than $650 million in the battle against cancer. And the type of cancer that claimed his life now has a cure rate of 80 percent and rarely requires amputations. Fox is a Canadian national hero.

FEARLESS FACTS

➲ **BORN:** July 28, 1958, Winnipeg, Manitoba, Canada ➲ **DIED:** June 28, 1981, New Westminster, British Columbia, Canada ➲ **OCCUPATION:** Long-distance runner ➲ **BOLDEST MOMENT:** Setting out on a cross-country Marathon of Hope to help fund a cure for cancer

JIM ABBOTT

BASEBALL'S NO-HIT WONDER

When Jim Abbott developed an interest in sports as a boy in Michigan, U.S.A., he was determined to play baseball with the other kids in his neighborhood. He wanted to be a pitcher. It was a bold choice for an athletic young man who'd been born without a right hand. With the help of his father, Abbott developed a special system for catching and throwing the ball, which he practiced by bouncing a rubber ball against the wall for hours.

His determination paid off. Abbott threw a no-hitter—or a game in which the other team scored no hits—in his first Little League game when he was 11. It would not be the last time. Abbott pitched for the American team at the 1988 Summer Olympics, helping beat Japan in the final game and winning a gold medal. While most professional baseball players begin their careers in the minor leagues, Abbott went from the Olympic team directly to Major League Baseball in 1989, when he was picked as a pitcher for the California Angels. He ended his first season as the Angels' Rookie of the Year.

Off the field, Abbott was a likable role model who was always quick to cast his missing hand as a strength rather than a weakness. On the field, until his retirement in 1999, he was one of the league's best pitchers. In 1993, while playing for the New York Yankees against the Cleveland Indians in a crucial championship game, he repeated the feat of his first Little League game: He pitched a no-hit victory.

"FIND SOMETHING YOU LOVE AND GO AFTER IT WITH ALL OF YOUR HEART."
—JIM ABBOTT

FEARLESS FACTS

→ **BORN:** September 19, 1967, Flint, Michigan, U.S.A. → **OCCUPATION:** Professional baseball player
→ **BOLDEST MOMENT:** Pitching a no-hitter in a championship game for the New York Yankees in 1993

MOMENT OF BRAVERY

He paddled out to his greatest challenge. How did this big-wave surfer ride into extreme-sports history?

THE SITUATION

Jeff Clark studied more than just math and English and history in high school. He studied sea monsters. They were created by storms more than a thousand miles away, appearing as barely visible bumps on the horizon before rearing up to a height of four stories and then crashing down in a spray of salty foam.

These were the monster waves of Mavericks, a surf break near San Francisco, California, U.S.A. Today, the spot is known as the Mount Everest of big-wave surfing, attracting professional surfers from around the world. But in the early 1970s, Mavericks was virtually unknown and considered too treacherous for surfing. The waves can reach 80 feet (24 m). Beneath them are jagged rocks, submerged caves, and worse. The break is a quarter of a mile (400 m) from shore in the middle of the Red Triangle, a breeding ground for great white sharks.

Clark, an avid surfer always eager for a larger wave and a bigger challenge, had studied Mavericks from his high school's seaside campus in Half Moon Bay, California. He had tried to persuade his pals to surf those savage swells peeling way, way off the coast, but they thought he was crazy. If he was going to ride Mavericks—and become a legend for discovering America's only big-wave surf spot outside of Hawaii—he'd have to do it alone.

THE MOMENT OF TRUTH

Fighting raging currents, 17-year-old Clark paddled out to the break for the first time in 1975. He felt alone, a tiny speck in a murky sea so cold that he would die quickly without his wet suit (which, incidentally, gave Clark the appearance of a great white's favorite snack: a sea lion). Soon enough, an incoming wave loomed like a mountain. Modern big-wave surfers clutch the tow ropes of zippy watercraft for a speed assist in catching a wave, but Clark built up speed the old-fashioned way: Putting down his head, he paddled, paddled, paddled with all his might down the wave's steepening face. Clark knew that speed was the key to surviving one of these beasts. Paddle too slowly and he risked getting sucked back up the wave and swallowed by its curling lip, then spun through the water like a sock in a washing machine.

When he felt his board begin to accelerate down the wave, Clark popped to his feet. An ominous shadow began creeping ahead of his board's nose. The wave's frothing crest was curling high above his head. If he didn't maintain his speed and steer clear, he wouldn't escape the crash zone. Tons of seawater would fall on his head and pin him to the rocky bottom. Cringing, Clark sunk low on his board to build speed and hoped for the best. The wave's lip crashed behind him in an explosion of foam. He'd made it! Clark had just become the first person to ride a Mavericks monster without sleeping with the fishes. He couldn't wait to share this discovery with the surfing world.

THE LEGACY

Clark surfed Mavericks for 15 years alone. For some strange reason, he couldn't talk his fellow surfers into paddling for 30 minutes through treacherous shark-infested waters for the opportunity to outrun waves the size of apartment buildings. Finally, in 1990, he persuaded two friends from nearby Santa Cruz to attempt the Mavericks break. They left feeling stoked. On the next good day, twelve surfers paddled into the lineup. The secret was out.

Today, extreme-sports athletes consider Clark a hero, surfing's equivalent of Sir Edmund Hillary (the first man to summit Mount Everest). Conquering his fears while respecting the ocean's power, he paddled into uncharted territory and proved that monsters could be tamed. Mavericks is one of the world's premiere big-wave surf spots, host of an annual contest with sponsors and cash prizes. Clark still surfs Mavericks, although now he's never alone.

CHAPTER FOUR

HEROES FOR HIRE

Movie stars get paid millions to put on costumes and play the roles of super-heroes in movies. Meanwhile, firefighters, police officers, and astronauts in the real world earn a lot less to act bravely on the job. This chapter is dedicated to those who work wonders at their work—and not just at the careers that we associate with requiring courage. Get ready to witness doctors, teachers, pilots, and even bus drivers go above and beyond their calls of duty.

Heroes of the New York City
Fire Department at the World
Trade Center site after the
attacks of September 11, 2001

NEIL ARMSTRONG

THE ORIGINAL MOONWALKER

The Apollo 11 moon lander was moments from making history in July 1969 when the mission's commander, Neil Armstrong, noticed a problem. The two-man spaceship had overshot its landing area and was approaching terrain too rugged for touch-down. Taking control from the craft's computers, an alarm sounding in his ears, Armstrong scanned the moon's cratered surface for a safe place to set down. Less than a minute's worth of fuel remained for the descent engine. If it dropped much lower, Armstrong would be ordered to abort the mission and ignite the ascent engine, rocketing the craft on a course back to Earth—and mission failure.

CRASH COURSE

A pilot since he was 16, Neil Armstrong built his career on quick thinking. As a Navy fighter pilot in the Korean War, he ejected from his plane after it was blasted by antiaircraft fire. He logged more than 900 flights in the world's most dangerous aircraft as a test pilot. Armstrong's closest call came during astronaut training. He was flying a moon-lander simulator when it began tilting out of control. Armstrong pulled the ejection handle and parachuted from

"THAT'S ONE SMALL STEP FOR MAN, ONE GIANT LEAP FOR MANKIND."
-NEIL ARMSTRONG, AS HE STEPPED ONTO THE SURFACE OF THE MOON

FEARLESS FACTS

➔ **BORN:** August 5, 1930, Wapakoneta, Ohio, U.S.A. ➔ **DIED:** August 25, 2012, Cincinnati, Ohio, U.S.A.
➔ **OCCUPATION:** Astronaut ➔ **BOLDEST MOMENT:** Stepping off the ladder of a spaceship and becoming the first human to visit another world

the crippled vehicle just 100 feet (30 m) from the ground. If he had delayed even half a second, his parachute wouldn't have opened in time.

TOUCHDOWN

Now, above the moon's surface, Armstrong's quick thinking was being put to the ultimate test. With hundreds of millions mesmerized back on Earth, he guided the module over the rocky ground until he found a safe landing spot. "Contact light," said copilot Buzz Aldrin. Probes on the lander's legs had touched the lunar surface. Armstrong shut down the engine and the ship settled gently on the surface of the moon. Twenty seconds of fuel remained.

As commander of the Apollo 11 mission, Armstrong had the honor of being the first human to walk on the moon's surface. But Apollo 11's mission was only half over. Less than a decade earlier, U.S. president John F. Kennedy had vowed that America would land humans on the moon and return them to Earth within the next decade. NASA had chosen Armstrong for this historic mission because of his piloting skill, quick thinking, and humility. He was "a reluctant hero who always believed he was just doing his job," Armstrong's family said when he passed away in 2012. Four days after they landed on the moon, Armstrong and Aldrin finished their job: Apollo 11 splashed down safely in the Pacific Ocean.

Apollo 11 launches from Kennedy Space Center, in Florida, U.S.A., on July 16, 1969.

Armstrong left the first human footprint on the surface of the moon (above).

TO BOLDLY GO
FIVE SPACE FIRSTS

Since before the dawn of civilization, humans have been lured over the horizon to find food, make a profit, or just to see what's beyond the mountains and oceans. By the middle of the last century, we aimed higher: outer space. Here are some voyagers who pioneered the final frontier.

FIRST HUMAN IN SPACE: Yuri Gagarin
(1934–1968)

Meet the first human to enter space. Although Yuri Gagarin was an astronaut for America's rivals in the Soviet Union's space program (which called its astronauts "cosmonauts"), he had much in common with Neil Armstrong: He came from humble beginnings, possessed incredible skill, and was praised for his humility. He was also exceedingly brave, exploring space when the technology was primitive and untested. When Gagarin returned to Earth after his history-making first spaceflight, for example, he had to parachute from his reentry capsule at 20,000 feet (6,096 m). Modern space shuttles, on the other hand, glide to a stop on a runway.

FIRST COMMERCIAL ASTRONAUT:
Mike Melvill (1940–)

Spectators craned their necks and shaded their eyes in 2004 to watch the speck of an experimental ship called SpaceShipOne zoom 62 miles (100 km) above California's Mojave Desert, officially soaring into the fringes of space. Why the hubbub over a feat that NASA has repeated routinely since the 1960s? Behind the controls sat veteran test pilot Michael Melvill. A co-owner of the company that built SpaceShipOne, he was about to make history as the first astronaut on a private spacecraft, or one not operated by a government agency. Before his historic trip to space, Melvill had flown just about every type of aircraft and held many aviation world records. His new record in commercial spaceflight—the next frontier of space travel—was literally out of this world.

FIRST CREW NEARLY LOST IN SPACE:
Apollo 13's Astronauts

Two days into Apollo 13's four-day voyage to the moon, in 1970, the three-man crew heard a big bang. Warning lights lit up, electrical systems shut down, and control thrusters sent the spacecraft shimmying through space 200,000 miles (322,000 km) from Earth. An electrical short had caused an oxygen tank to explode. Suddenly, Commander Jim Lovell and his crewmates, Jack Swigert and Fred Haise, had a new mission: survival. They didn't have enough air and electricity to make it home, let alone to the moon. Using the moon lander as a lifeboat, the astronauts shut down all unnecessary systems—including heat—to conserve power. They fired the lander's engine to boost their speed and shave hours off their return trip—hours they couldn't afford to waste in space. Engineers back on Earth sprang into action, pooling their impressive brainpower to improvise solutions to a host of life-threatening problems, including a buildup of deadly carbon dioxide inside the lander. Finally, after nearly four days of around-the-clock ingenuity, the Apollo 13 crew arrived safely back on Earth.

FIRST ASTRONAUT IN SPACE FOR MORE THAN A YEAR: Valeri Polyakov (1942–)

Space is a dangerous place: More than 20 astronauts have died doing their job. Radiation, muscle loss from lack of gravity, and tiny meteorites that move faster than a bullet are some of the many hazards that astronauts face while on the job. To prove that humans can survive far from home, cosmonaut Valeri Polyakov spent a record 438 days—longer than it would take to travel to Mars—aboard the Russian Mir space station in the mid-1990s. He returned to Earth a little wobbly but otherwise healthy, paving the way for manned exploration of our solar system.

GUTSY GALS

FIRST AMERICAN WOMAN IN SPACE: Sally Ride (1951–2012)

5-4-3-2-1 ... we have liftoff! On June 18, 1983, Sally Ride became the first American woman to travel to space. At 32, she was also the youngest astronaut to go to space, a record that stands today. While earning her Ph.D. in astrophysics at Stanford University in California, U.S.A., Ride had seen a newspaper ad calling for applicants to the astronaut program. Ride flew at the chance. Since her barrier-breaking flight, 39 female NASA astronauts have blasted off into space. Ride went on to open doors for other women in science. In 2001, she founded Sally Ride Science, an organization that aims to inspire students—especially girls and minorities—to study the STEM subjects of science, technology, engineering, and math.

JAY JONAS AND THE FIREFIGHTERS OF LADDER 6

A COMPANY OF HEROES

The men of Ladder Company 6, a firefighter company from New York City's Chinatown, were rushing up an emergency stairwell of the World Trade Center's north tower on September 11, 2001, when they felt the floor begin to quake. Lights flickered overhead. Captain Jay Jonas, the ladder company's leader, heard the news over his radio: The neighboring south tower had just collapsed! Fearing the north tower would follow suit, Jonas ordered his men to turn around and head for the exit. On the 20th floor, they encountered a 59-year-old bookkeeper named Josephine Harris, who had just descended 50 floors on her own. She was out of breath and barely able to stand. If the men slowed to help her down the stairs, they risked their own lives. But they were firefighters, and saving people was their job. Jonas ordered his men to help her. Minutes later, the world came crashing down on them all: The north tower had just collapsed above them.

Amazingly, the men of Ladder Company 6 survived because of their heroism rather than in spite of it. The six firefighters and Harris were covered in concrete dust and up to their knees in debris, but they were alive. Miraculously, they had landed in a tiny pocket of safety in Stairwell B. The floors above were in ruin. The stairwell below was a snarl of twisted steel and jagged concrete. If the firefighters hadn't slowed to help Harris, they would have been crushed in the floors below. They had saved Harris and she had saved them. She became known as the Angel of Ladder Company 6.

> "IF SOMEBODY NEEDS HELP, WE GOT TO GIVE IT A SHOT."
> —JAY JONAS, CAPTAIN OF LADDER COMPANY 6 ON SEPTEMBER 11, 2001

FEARLESS FACTS

➔ **OCCUPATION:** New York City firefighters ➔ **BOLDEST MOMENT:** Slowing to rescue a woman from a building on the verge of collapse

RICK RESCORLA

THE LAST MAN TO LEAVE

A British-born retired Army officer, Rick Rescorla was a vice president of security for financial company Morgan Stanley, the largest tenant in New York City's World Trade Center. He had been working at the north tower when it was bombed in 1993 and had helped people evacuate the damaged building. He believed a similar attack could happen again and that the next time might be worse. On September 11, he was ready.

But Rescorla was a hero long before 2001. During the war in Vietnam in the 1960s, he steadied the nerves of the young soldiers under his command by singing English folk songs in between giving orders. He retired from the U.S. Army with many medals, including the Silver Star, earned for bravery. In 1994, he faced a new foe: cancer. Rescorla was undergoing painful treatment for the disease when the attacks occurred on September 11.

Grabbing a bullhorn, in his strong and assuring voice, Rescorla ordered the Morgan Stanley employees to leave the building. His co-workers knew exactly what to do—Rescorla had been practicing safety drills with them for years. To keep his co-workers calm in the stairwell, Rescorla sang the same English songs he had once crooned to boost the morale of his comrades in the Vietnam War. He led nearly 2,700 Morgan Stanley employees to safety—almost all of them, spread out over 22 floors—before the towers collapsed. Rescorla didn't want to leave until he was sure everyone had escaped. He was last seen on the 10th floor of the south tower heading upstairs, looking for more people to save.

"IT CANNOT BE EVER SAID YE FOR THE BATTLE WERE NOT READY; STAND AND NEVER YIELD!"
—FROM A SONG SUNG BY RICK RESCORLA TO CALM HIS CO-WORKERS

FEARLESS FACTS

➲ **BORN:** May 27, 1939, Cornwall, England ➲ **DIED:** September 11, 2001, New York, New York, U.S.A.
➲ **OCCUPATION:** Vice president of security for Morgan Stanley ➲ **BOLDEST MOMENT:** Leading thousands of colleagues to safety from the World Trade Center

ORDINARY HEROES
BRAVERY AT EVERYDAY JOBS

Danger is a daily part of the job for police officers, firemen, and astronauts, but these four workplace heroes probably didn't think they'd need to put their lives on the line while on the clock. These (extra)ordinary people put themselves in harm's way—in the path of fire, criminals, radiation, and nature's fury—and risked it all to help others.

SMOOTH OPERATOR: Joseph Zito (1883–1932)

The fire began in a bin of fabric scraps. Within minutes, it was raging through the Triangle Shirtwaist Factory, a New York City garment manufacturer staffed by hundreds of young immigrant workers in 1911. With emergency exits locked and fire escapes falling apart, the fire became one of the deadliest industrial disasters in American history. But it would have been even deadlier if not for an elevator operator named Joseph Zito.

Along with fellow operator Gaspar Mortillalo, Zito rode his elevator through smoke and flames to the ninth floor. With fire licking at their heels, panicked workers flooded Zito's car, nearly crushing him in the process. Zito made the ascent three times until the elevator shaft became too damaged for another trip. He's credited with saving nearly 150 people—most of them young women—from a fire that claimed almost as many lives.

BRAVERY ON THE BUS: Tim Watson

When a young man with a toddler boarded his bus in California, U.S.A., in June 2015, driver Tim Watson didn't think much about it at first. But when news of the recent kidnapping of a three-year-old boy came through his onboard communications system about 15 minutes later, he connected the descriptions of the suspect and the child to the two riders. Keeping his cool, Watson quickly hatched a plan: He told his passengers that he needed to stop the vehicle to search for a missing backpack. He then pulled over and began to make his way toward the rear of the bus, where the two were sitting, so he could get a closer look at the child and his alleged kidnapper to see if they indeed matched the police descriptions. When he saw that they did, Watson quietly called the police. Officers met the bus at the next stop and rescued the boy, who was reunited with his grateful parents. Watson, meanwhile, was hailed as a hero by police for his quick thinking and bravery.

DANGER ZONE: Yasuteru Yamada (1939–)

Seventy-two might seem a late age to apply for a new job, but Yasuteru Yamada—a retired engineer living in Tokyo—had heroic reasons for seeking employment at Japan's Fukushima nuclear power plant in 2011. Just weeks before, an earthquake and tsunami of destructive waves had rocked this seaside Japanese facility, triggering the worst nuclear accident in 25 years. Half of the plant's six reactors were damaged, leaking deadly radiation into the surrounding countryside and nearby ocean. Workers sent to secure the reactors and clean up the plant faced the danger of developing cancer from exposure to the radiation. The job had become a suicide mission.

So Yamada asked if he could do the work instead. As a former engineer at a steel plant, he had the technical skills necessary to repair the plant. And because radiation-related illnesses can take years to develop, Yamada figured that older workers had less to lose than younger ones. Together with a fellow retired engineer, Yamada recruited about 400 volunteers over 60—including an 82-year-old man—to spare Fukushima's young workers from the deadly cleanup job.

CALM BEFORE THE STORM: Rhonda Crosswhite

GUTSY GALS

More than a mile (1.6 km) wide and packing winds exceeding 200 miles an hour (322 km/h), the tornado that touched down outside the town of Moore, Oklahoma, U.S.A., in May 2013 shredded houses and tossed cars. Plaza Towers Elementary School sat directly in its path. Nothing stood between the school's fifth graders and the storm's fury except flimsy walls and Rhonda Crosswhite, the social studies teacher.

Without thinking twice, Crosswhite led six students into a bathroom stall and hunkered over them, using her body as a shield against the tornado bearing down on their school. Over the roar of the storm, with debris raining on her back, Crosswhite kept telling the students not to worry, that they would be fine. When the tornado finally passed, the students looked up to see a stormy sky where the roof used to be. They were all fine. Crosswhite had shielded her students from one of the most powerful forces on Earth.

NERVES OF STEEL

If extreme heights make your stomach lurch, then you're probably wondering how the men in this picture avoid losing their lunch. The famous shot shows construction workers eating on the 69th floor of an unfinished skyscraper, their legs dangling 840 feet (256 m) above New York City streets. The image raises so many questions. Why is no one wearing a safety harness? Are these men courageous or just crazy?

Maybe a bit of both. The photo was taken in 1932, during a period of economic hardship called the Great Depression. Americans were desperate for work. Clipping on safety harnesses and inching across the iron bones of buildings took time, and time cost the owners money. Cautious workers were shown the door and replaced with men willing to work faster despite the higher risks. And although the photo here was posed for a publicity stunt, high-rise builders still clambered through the sky without harnesses or other protective gear. The job was not for the timid.

And it cost lives. Eleven men fell to their deaths building San Francisco's Golden Gate Bridge in the 1930s. Five workers died constructing the Empire State Building. The men in this photo were a cautious as well as courageous crew. The death toll for their building, known as the RCA Building when it was built: zero.

Construction work is safer today, thanks to new safety regulations. But according to U.S. labor statistics, it's still the most dangerous sector of industry—even more dangerous than firefighting and police work. Workers risk injury or death from accidental falls, road accidents while driving monstrous vehicles, and wielding heavy machinery. It's a deadly job, but somebody has to do it. These men rise to the challenge.

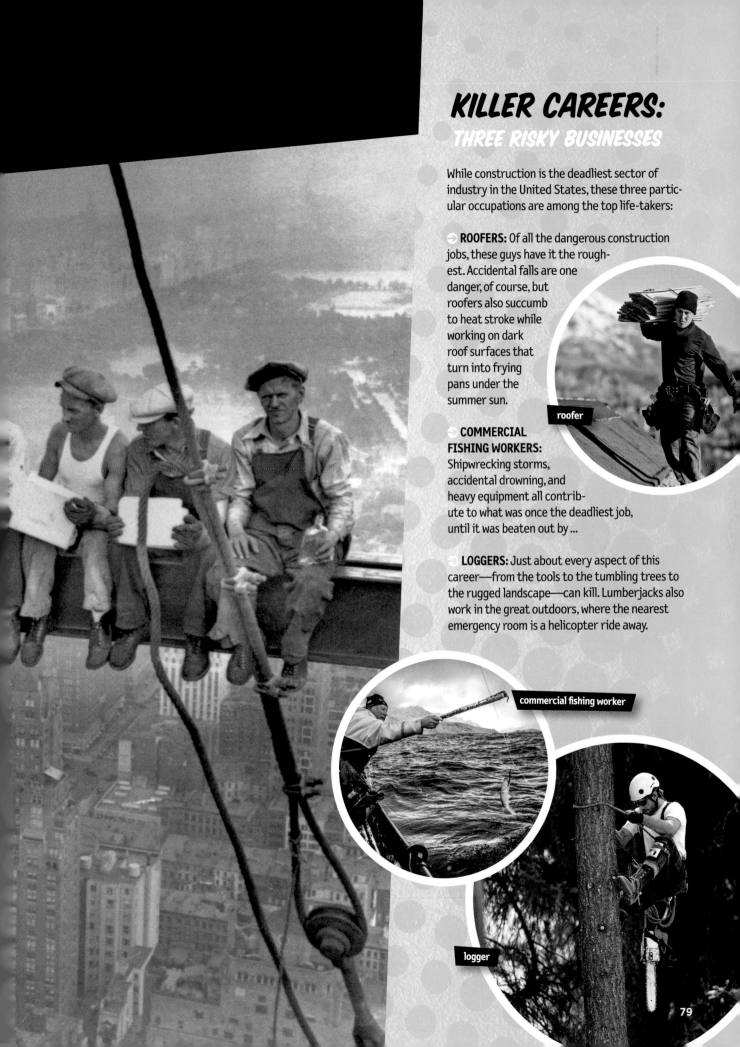

KILLER CAREERS:
THREE RISKY BUSINESSES

While construction is the deadliest sector of industry in the United States, these three particular occupations are among the top life-takers:

➔ **ROOFERS:** Of all the dangerous construction jobs, these guys have it the roughest. Accidental falls are one danger, of course, but roofers also succumb to heat stroke while working on dark roof surfaces that turn into frying pans under the summer sun.

roofer

➔ **COMMERCIAL FISHING WORKERS:** Shipwrecking storms, accidental drowning, and heavy equipment all contribute to what was once the deadliest job, until it was beaten out by ...

➔ **LOGGERS:** Just about every aspect of this career—from the tools to the tumbling trees to the rugged landscape—can kill. Lumberjacks also work in the great outdoors, where the nearest emergency room is a helicopter ride away.

commercial fishing worker

logger

CHESLEY "SULLY" SULLENBERGER

THE PILOT WHO KEPT HIS COOL

Flight 1549—a US Airways jetliner carrying 155 people—was barely off the runway on January 15, 2009, when passengers and crew heard a thump and then ... silence. The engines had stopped! A flock of geese had flown into the path of the plane, crippling it less than two minutes after its takeoff from LaGuardia Airport in New York, U.S.A. Only 3,000 feet (914 m) above a bustling area, the 74-ton (67-t) plane had suddenly become a giant glider—one that was losing speed and altitude. The crew didn't have time to turn around and land at LaGuardia or reach the safety of nearby airports. If they didn't act immediately, their plane would crash.

THE RIGHT STUFF

Fortunately for the passengers, Captain Chesley "Sully" Sullenberger was in command. An airline pilot since 1980, he had decades of experience and had even worked as a crash investigator. Before that, he had been a fighter pilot for the U.S. Air Force, serving as a squadron leader and flight instructor. He had learned from experience what could go wrong while piloting an airplane. More importantly, he knew how to make things right.

And yet in more than 40 years of flying, Sullenberger had never encountered an emergency like this—not even in training simulators. While his copilot reviewed

"WE MAY END UP IN THE HUDSON." —CAPTAIN "SULLY" SULLENBERGER

FEARLESS FACTS

➜ **BORN:** January 23, 1951, Denison, Texas, U.S.A. ➜ **OCCUPATION:** Airline pilot, lecturer
➜ **BOLDEST MOMENT:** Accomplishing a daring water landing of his seemingly doomed jet, saving everyone aboard

emergency procedures, Sully calmly scanned for a safe place to land as buildings and streets grew closer through the cockpit windows. With no time—or altitude—to spare, he made a daring decision: He would land the plane in the Hudson River.

Airline passengers line the wings of the downed plane and wait to be rescued (above); firefighters assist with the rescue of passengers (above left).

MIRACLE ON THE HUDSON

Anyone who turned on the TV that afternoon was in for a shocking sight: News reports featuring a massive passenger jet bobbing in the icy waters of the Hudson River. Flight attendants on board helped passengers to the emergency exits, where they climbed atop the wings and into rafts to await rescue. Miraculously, Sullenberger had glided the plane over the George Washington Bridge before setting it down gently in the water. He even brought it to a stop near a ferry terminal so that boats nearby could pluck the passengers to safety. The last person to leave Flight 1549, Sullenberger checked the aisles twice to make sure everyone had gotten out. His passengers owed their lives to Sully's decades of training and experience. "One way of looking at this might be that, for 42 years, I've been making small, regular deposits in this bank of experience, education, and training," he told news anchor Katie Couric after the incident. "And on January 15, the balance was sufficient so that I could make a very large withdrawal."

THE FIRST POLICEWOMAN:
Alice Stebbins Wells (1873–1957)

GUTSY GALS

In the early 20th century, there were almost no women in law enforcement. The few females on the police force weren't officers; they were matrons who cared for female prisoners. Los Angeles social worker Alice Stebbins Wells successfully petitioned her city government to change the rules and, in 1910, she became a Los Angeles Police Department (LAPD) officer and the nation's first policewoman. Wells, who hand-stitched her own uniform, received a special badge from the LAPD that read "Policewoman's Badge Number One." Throughout her career, Wells visited cities nationwide to encourage other women to join the police force. By 1937, the LAPD employed 39 policewomen.

CRASH TESTED
FIVE COURAGEOUS CREWMEN

When disaster strikes by land, air, or sea, there is little time to formulate a plan and put it into action. Often it's the resourcefulness, savvy, and bravery of the crew—and even the passengers—that stands between life and death. Meet five fast-thinking professionals who faced unthinkable challenges and kept a cool head during a crisis.

HEAVY METTLE: Casey Jones (1863–1900)

In 1900, when steam-powered locomotives were the fastest way to travel across the United States, John Luther "Casey" Jones drove them the fastest. The engineer of the Cannonball Express passenger train, he had a reputation for keeping his trains on schedule. All his skills were put to the test on the soggy, foggy night of April 30, 1900, when Jones, going 75 miles an hour (121 km/h) around a blind corner, came upon a stalled freight train in Mississippi, U.S.A. With lightning-quick reflexes, he yanked the brakes and sounded his train's whistle to warn the people ahead. Jones managed to cut the Cannonball's speed in half before it collided with the freight train, saving all of his passengers. He died in the crash with one hand on the brake and the other on the whistle, according to legend.

GUITAR HERO: Moss Hills

Chairs and tables tumbled across the dining room while seawater gurgled up from the lower decks. Passengers were beginning to panic. Their ship was sinking! As the Greek cruise ship *Oceanos* pitched and rolled like an angry beast through stormy seas off South Africa in 1991, Moss Hills ran to the bridge to talk to the captain—only to find the bridge was abandoned. Hills called for help on the radio. The captain of a nearby ship answered, asking for Moss's rank. "I'm a guitarist!" Moss replied. Many of the *Oceanos*'s crew had already boarded lifeboats, leaving the ship's musician (along with his wife and other members of the entertainment staff) in charge of helping the passengers. Moss's Mayday summoned rescue helicopters and other ships. All 571 passengers aboard were saved, and Moss was one of the last to leave.

SPIRIT IN THE SKY: Mike Nerandzic
(1961–2011)

Australian pilot Michael Nerandzic's 26 years of experience flying airships helped save the lives of his passengers in 2011. He was landing a Goodyear blimp at an airfield in Germany when his engine caught fire. Thinking fast, Nerandzic descended to within a few feet of the airfield and shouted for his three passengers to hop out, although he knew the airship would launch skyward from the sudden loss of weight. With the passengers safely on the ground, Nerandzic guided the flaming blimp up and away from his ground crew before perishing in the crash.

STRONG-ARM TACTICS: Nigel Ogden

British Airways Flight 5390 had climbed just past 17,000 feet (5,182 m) into clear skies in June 1990 when the unthinkable happened: A panel of the cockpit's windshield blew loose in an explosion of mist and frigid wind. The sudden loss of pressure sucked the pilot from his seat and almost completely out the window. Flight attendant Nigel Ogden grabbed the pilot by his belt and held him in place as long as he could, with other crew members assisting throughout the terrifying ordeal; the copilot managed to land the plane safely. The pilot survived with some arm fractures and a broken thumb; Ogden suffered a dislocated shoulder and some frostbite from the freezing air but was otherwise physically unhurt.

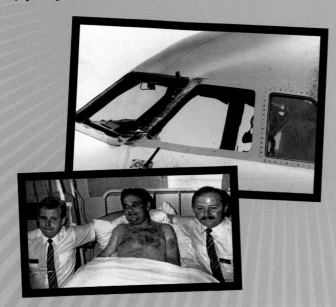

DERRING-DO ON DECK:
Charles John Joughin
(1878–1956)

When the passenger ship *Titanic* struck an iceberg on the night of April 14, 1912, and began slowly sinking into the North Atlantic, Englishman Charles John Joughin rose to the occasion without going down with the ship. Springing to action, he threw deck chairs into the water as additional flotation devices, made sure fleeing passengers had food, and refused his assigned seat on a lifeboat. Joughin went into the icy water but miraculously managed to survive until he was plucked to safety. He went on to live another 44 years.

WILLIAM SHAKESPEARE

THE BLOCKBUSTER BARD

"SOME ARE BORN GREAT, SOME ACHIEVE GREATNESS, AND SOME HAVE GREATNESS THRUST UPON 'EM."
—MALVOLIO IN TWELFTH NIGHT

The king is dead, murdered by a wicked brother who takes control of the kingdom. The king's son, the prince, is forced to flee to a neighboring land, where the ghost of his father urges him to retake his realm. Sound familiar? That's the plot of Disney's *The Lion King*, released in 1994. It's also the plot of *Hamlet*, written by English playwright and poet William Shakespeare around the year 1600. Some historians argue that *Hamlet* is the greatest of Shakespeare's nearly 40 plays. Few could deny that Shakespeare is history's greatest writer of the English language.

Yet little is known about the man who would become England's national poet. His family was well off but not wealthy, earning enough to send young Shakespeare to a school that focused on history, poetry, and writing. He married when he was 18 and had two children, but the details of his life afterward are lost until the 1590s. That's when he started making his mark as a playwright and actor.

Stage productions were as popular in Shakespeare's time—especially with everyday Londoners—as movies are today, and the playwright produced one crowd-pleaser after another. Shakespeare also wrote poems called sonnets that tackled the themes of the day: exploration, betrayal, love, and war. His work made him wealthy but not famous. That came much later, starting in the 19th century, when the world began to marvel at Shakespeare's wit and way with language. He coined more than 2,000 newfangled words that are still fashionable today, including the words "newfangled" and "fashionable."

FEARLESS FACTS

➜ **BORN:** ca 1564, Stratford-Upon-Avon, England ➜ **DIED:** April 23, 1616, Stratford-Upon-Avon, England
➜ **OCCUPATION:** Playwright and poet ➜ **BOLDEST MOMENT:** Writing plays and poems that have inspired modern storytelling

FREDERICK DOUGLASS

FROM SLAVE TO INSPIRATION

Frederick Douglass was born a slave. Education was forbidden for most children in his circumstance, but young Douglass sneaked lessons from white children who attended school nearby. He knew that his most powerful tool was knowledge, and he wanted to share it with other slaves.

Some plantation owners hated the idea of their slaves getting an education. They attacked Douglass and those he taught. Realizing he could never battle slavery as a slave, Douglass escaped to the safety of New York in 1838.

A writer with the power to move people, Douglass became a leader of the abolitionist movement, an organized effort in the northern states to end slavery. He traveled throughout the North and Midwest telling of his life on the plantation. Mobs jeered and attacked him. But Douglass's abolitionist friends urged him to write a book about his experiences. The more people learned of the horrors of slavery, abolitionists figured, the more people would turn against it. Douglass published his autobiography in 1845.

His writing fueled the growing resentment of slavery, which culminated in 1861 with the beginning of the Civil War between the northern states and the slave-owning southern states. Douglass advised President Abraham Lincoln on many issues, such as allowing black soldiers to fight for their freedom. After the end of the war and the abolition of slavery, Douglass continued to advocate for causes he believed in—including the expansion of rights for African Americans and women—until his death in 1895.

"IF THERE IS NO STRUGGLE, THERE IS NO PROGRESS."
—FREDERICK DOUGLASS

FEARLESS FACTS

➡ **BORN:** ca 1818, Talbot County, Maryland, U.S.A. ➡ **DIED:** February 20, 1895, Washington, D.C., U.S.A.
➡ **OCCUPATION:** Author, civil rights leader, and speaker ➡ **BOLDEST MOMENT:** Speaking against the evils of slavery despite threats from angry mobs

MOMENT OF BRAVERY

These heroes refused to abandon their post during a natural disaster, despite the great danger of staying. How did their courage save lives?

THE SITUATION

Streets cracked. Power poles toppled. Buildings swayed. The earthquake that struck off the coast of Japan in 2011 was one of the most powerful ever recorded. In many parts of the country, the ground shook like the deck of a ship tossed in a titanic storm. But when the shaking finally subsided, the danger had only just begun for many seaside towns.

Manning the emergency loudspeakers in the fishing village of Minamisanriku was 52-year-old Takeshi Miura, who had begun urging townspeople to head for higher ground as soon as the quake struck. He was joined by Miki Endo, a 24-year-old newlywed woman and fellow official in the three-story Disaster Control Center. Both were trained to deal with earthquakes. It was their job to warn the town's residents of a more terrifying beast bearing down on them. "A 10-meter [33-foot] tsunami is expected," Miura said over the loudspeakers with Endo at his side. "Please evacuate to higher ground."

THE MOMENT OF TRUTH

One of the most destructive forces on the planet, tsunamis are spawned by coastal or undersea earthquakes, volcanoes, and even asteroid impacts. Such earthshaking events displace ocean water around or above them, triggering rolling waves that zoom across the ocean at the speed of a passenger jet. When these waves reach shallow waters, they undergo a terrifying transformation. Walls of water as high as 100 feet (30 m) slosh ashore and rage over the land, washing away entire towns.

Just 30 minutes after the earthquake struck off the Japanese coast, its killer tsunami wave had reached the barrier built to protect Minamisanriku. The wave was more than four stories high—high enough to crash over the barrier and barrel through the lower floors of Miura and Endo's nearby Disaster Control Center. As the tsunami crested the town's barrier, co-workers urged Miura and Endo to seek the safety of their building's roof. Both refused to leave their posts. Miura insisted on making one more announcement, warning residents that the tsunami had reached the city. Endo was seen clutching the microphone as the killer wave struck the building.

THE LEGACY

The 2011 earthquake off of Japan unleashed a tsunami with waves topping 133 feet (41 m), killing more than 15,000 people across the country. When Miura's wife heard her husband's confident voice issuing tsunami warnings over the town's loud-speakers, she immediately headed for the safety of a nearby mountain. Endo's mother was at a fish farm on the coast when she heard her daughter's warnings. She fled for higher ground. Both survived the killer wave because of Miura's and Endo's messages. Unfortunately, the duo were among the nearly 800 Minamisanriku residents washed away. Their decision to stay at their posts saved thousands but cost them their own lives. Today, the two officials are national heroes. Endo's tale is even taught in school: a lesson in heroism and sacrifice.

CHAPTER FIVE

PEACE HEROES

Some of the bravest humans in history wielded words, wisdom, and charm instead of weapons. When few dared to speak against intolerance and bigotry, they stood for truth and justice—becoming targets for those who would cling to hate. These are the champions of peace, fighting for civil rights and making the world a better place for all. Many lost their lives. For some, the struggle still continues today.

Dr. Martin Luther King, Jr., at the 1963 March
on Washington for Jobs and Freedom

MARTIN LUTHER KING, JR.

HE HAD A DREAM FOR JUSTICE AND EQUALITY

He took the podium on the steps of the Lincoln Memorial and looked upon a sea of faces both black and white. Organizers expected about 100,000 people to participate in this March on Washington, a rally in 1963 against the unfair treatment of black people in America. Some 250,000 filled every inch of lawn around the Lincoln Memorial Reflecting Pool as Dr. Martin Luther King, Jr.—a key figure in the crusade against racial discrimination—prepared to deliver the day's climactic speech. Thousands fell silent as he began talking in a strong voice honed from his years as a pastor and civil rights leader. What he said next changed history.

FIRST VICTORY

Growing up under the Jim Crow laws of the South (see sidebar), young Martin Luther King, Jr., experienced the injustice of segregation and bigotry. But he was a hardworking student, and by 15 he had skipped two grades and started college. By 25, King had earned a Ph.D. and become a minister like his father. He saw the enormous gulfs between the "inalienable rights" mentioned in the Declaration of Independence and the segregated lives of black people in the South.

> "THE ARC OF THE MORAL UNIVERSE IS LONG, BUT IT BENDS TOWARD JUSTICE."
> -DR. MARTIN LUTHER KING, JR.

FEARLESS FACTS

→ **BORN:** January 15, 1929, Atlanta, Georgia, U.S.A. → **DIED:** April 4, 1968, Memphis, Tennessee, U.S.A.
→ **OCCUPATION:** Minister, leader of the civil rights movement → **BOLDEST MOMENT:** Helping lead approximately 250,000 people to the Lincoln Memorial in 1963 for a peaceful civil rights demonstration

When a black woman named Rosa Parks was arrested in 1955 for not giving up her bus seat to a white passenger in Montgomery, Alabama, U.S.A., King called on all black people in the city to refuse to use public transportation. This was a courageous stand. Boycotters endured abuse as they walked to work every day; King's house was even bombed. But they kept up the boycott for more than a year and challenged the city to a legal battle after a 1956 U.S. Supreme Court ruling declared that segregation was illegal. Finally, Montgomery ended segregation on public transportation. The modern civil rights movement had its first major victory.

UNDER ATTACK

But this was just in one city. King wanted to improve civil rights for black people throughout the South. Together with other ministers and activists, he formed the Southern Christian Leadership Conference in 1957. They staged demonstrations and meetings to help register black voters and to battle what was now illegal segregation. Despite facing constant threats and intimidation, King insisted on a strategy of passive resistance: nonviolent protests such as marches and sit-ins. For instance, protesters would sit at whites-only restaurant tables until they were either served or arrested.

King was arrested dozens of times for staging peaceful protests. Police in southern cities that clung to segregation beat protesters. Photos and footage of the attacks and arrests outraged black and white Americans across the country. Millions of Americans rallied behind the civil rights movement.

KING'S SPEECH

"I have a dream today," King said at the 1963 March on Washington. "I have a dream that my four little children will one day live in a nation where they will not be judged by the color of their skin but by the content of their character." His words stirred a nation. A year later, the U.S. Congress passed the Civil Rights Act, which outlawed discrimination and racial segregation in schools and in the workplace. That same year, King won the Nobel Peace Prize, one of the highest honors in the world.

King and his wife, Coretta, marching in Alabama in 1965

SHADOW OF SLAVERY

The U.S. Civil War may have ended slavery in 1865, but black Americans still faced terrible treatment in the United States—particularly in the South. Despite a series of amendments to the U.S. Constitution guaranteeing black people citizenship and the right to vote, a system of segregation began taking shape in the late 1800s. In the South, Jim Crow laws restricted black people to their own restaurants and restrooms, schools, pools, beaches, and churches. These places were supposed to be "separate but equal" but rarely were. Imagine being forced to use a broken-down water fountain or give up your seat on the bus to other passengers just because of the color of your skin.

In the North, segregation was not the law but it was still common. In all parts of the country, black people who stood up for their civil rights—the right to vote and receive equal treatment—were threatened by violence. Many were killed. Jim Crow laws and intimidation made it difficult and dangerous for black people to vote and bring about a better life. The situation seemed hopeless, and yet black people found the courage to defy authorities who were morally wrong.

KING'S MEN
ALLIES IN THE CIVIL RIGHTS MOVEMENT

Martin Luther King, Jr., was an inspirational and charismatic force in the fight for civil rights, but he was far from alone in the struggle. Meet the heroes who paved the path to equality, provided inspiration, devised the strategies, and carried on the fight ...

THE SPIRITUAL MENTOR: Benjamin Mays
(1894–1984)

Young Benjamin Mays never forgot the day he saw a mob of white men threaten to beat his father—a former slave—just because he wanted to vote. Growing up in South Carolina, U.S.A., Mays dared to speak out against segregation before the civil rights movement solidified under the leadership of his star pupil: Martin Luther King, Jr. Mays was ordained as a minister and earned a Ph.D. before becoming the president of Morehouse College in Atlanta, Georgia, U.S.A. When King began classes at Morehouse in 1944, Mays became his mentor, instilling in King the value of human dignity and racial equality. Mays helped the young minister believe he could make a difference.

THE CONGRESSMAN: John Lewis (1940–)

While growing up in the Deep South, where black people were terrorized for not "knowing their place," young John Lewis was warned by his parents to stay out of trouble. He didn't listen. Lewis got into what he calls "necessary trouble" after seeing the success of the Montgomery bus boycotts. Authorities in the South resorted to all sorts of dirty tricks to keep black people from voting. Lewis and hundreds of other protesters were beaten by state police while leading a march for voting rights near Selma, Alabama, U.S.A., in 1965. News footage showing the unprovoked police brutality of "Bloody Sunday" helped speed up the passage of the Voting Rights Act of 1965. Lewis continued to push for voting rights and was elected to the U.S. House of Representatives in 1986. Today, he is one of the most respected members of Congress.

THE RIGHT-HAND MAN: Ralph D. Abernathy
(1926–1990)

When Martin Luther King, Jr., organized the Montgomery bus boycotts, this fellow Baptist minister was there to help. When racist terrorists damaged King's house with a bomb to intimidate him, they bombed Abernathy's house as well. When King was arrested for civil disobedience, Abernathy went to jail with him. The two men had a friendship forged by fire and strengthened by a common cause. They co-founded the Southern Christian Leadership Conference, with King as president and Abernathy as his vice president. They organized peaceful marches and sit-ins together and were rarely photographed apart. When King was shot by an assassin in 1968, Abernathy was at his side. He had to carry on the struggle without his best friend and greatest ally.

THE STRATEGIST: Bayard Rustin
(1912–1987)

A black and openly gay man who refused to fight in World War II for religious reasons, Bayard Rustin got a triple dose of discrimination in the 1940s. Despite constant threats and several arrests, he was a tireless advocate for human rights and a pioneer in the civil rights movement, organizing protests against segregation. He was a seasoned organizer and civil rights strategist by the time he met Martin Luther King, Jr., in the 1950s. Rustin advised King to rely on the same nonviolent strategies as Indian activist Mohandas Gandhi (see page 96). Rustin was instrumental in organizing the 1963 March on Washington and one of King's finest hours, the "I Have a Dream" speech.

THE PIVOTAL PROTESTER: Rosa Parks (1913–2005)

GUTSY GALS

Her refusal to give up her bus seat to a white passenger on December 1, 1955, sparked the first large-scale protest against segregation, but Rosa Parks's story didn't stop there. After the Montgomery bus boycott spurred the U.S. Supreme Court to rule in 1956 that bus segregation was unconstitutional, Parks was fired from her job, and she and her husband had to leave Alabama in 1957 because of threats to their safety. But she continued to work for civil rights for the rest of her life. Her act of courage helped inspire the beginning of the civil rights movement in the United States and became a symbol of the fight for equality.

THE LITTLE ROCK NINE

A DIFFERENT KIND OF CLASS WARFARE

For nine black students trying to attend Little Rock Central High School in Arkansas, U.S.A., in 1957, going to class required incredible courage—and a military escort. Three years before, the U.S. Supreme Court had ruled that school segregation was unconstitutional, ordering schools to desegregate as quickly as possible. Arkansas governor Orval Faubus refused. In response, the National Association for the Advancement of Colored People registered nine high-achieving black students (later known as the Little Rock Nine) to enter the largest all-white school in Arkansas' capital city.

The students, ranging in age from 15 to 17, were Minnijean Brown, Elizabeth Eckford, Ernest Green, Thelma Mothershed, Melba Patillo, Gloria Ray, Terrence Roberts, Jefferson Thomas, and Carlotta Walls. When they showed up on the first day of class in September 1957, they had to walk a gauntlet of angry white protesters. The mob spat at the students, shouting threatening and racist comments. When they reached the school's door, the black students were turned away by National Guard soldiers following the governor's orders.

When the Little Rock Nine returned nearly three weeks later with an escort of U.S. Army soldiers ordered by President Dwight Eisenhower, they finally entered the school. Yet their ordeal was far from over. They endured bullying and racist jeers from white students; one of the nine described each day as a "hellish torture chamber." But the Little Rock Nine persevered and finished the school year.

> "I WAS DETERMINED TO FINISH THAT YEAR. I WAS NOT GOING TO GIVE UP."
> —CARLOTTA WALLS LANIER OF THE LITTLE ROCK NINE

FEARLESS FACTS

→ **OCCUPATION:** High school students → **BOLDEST MOMENT:** Facing down racist mobs as the first black students to attend a segregated school

THE CHILDREN OF BIRMINGHAM

STUDENTS UNDER ATTACK

They were blasted to the sidewalk by fire hoses. Police sicced dogs on them. Many were thrown in jail. And they were all children, some as young as six years old. In May 1963, roughly 3,000 black schoolchildren filled the streets of Birmingham, Alabama, U.S.A., to stage nonviolent protests against segregation in their city. The police, led by Commissioner Bull Connor, were ready to stop them.

Birmingham was considered America's most segregated city at the time, the focal point of Dr. Martin Luther King, Jr.'s civil rights movement. It was a dangerous place for black people, who faced threats and physical violence from members of the Ku Klux Klan, a white-supremacy group. Black protesters risked losing their jobs, which were already difficult to come by in the racist South. But kids didn't have jobs to lose. King, after much consideration, approved a plan to recruit thousands of courageous students from schools in and around Birmingham to march on the city in early May. The boys and girls were eager to stand against the injustice they faced every day. They met at 16th Street Baptist Church, a rallying point for the movement (it was bombed later that year by racist terrorists) before setting out.

Connor unleashed his police on the students. Fortunately, reporters were there to witness what happened next. White and black Americans were appalled at the brutality of what they saw, and Connor was fired from his position as police commissioner. The Children's Crusade of 1963 became a defining moment in the fight for civil rights.

NEWSPAPERS ACROSS THE COUNTRY RAN SHOCKING PHOTOS OF POLICE ATTACKING STUDENTS AND LEADING THEM TO JAIL.

FEARLESS FACTS

➔ **OCCUPATION:** Students ➔ **BOLDEST MOMENT:** Marching for civil rights despite the threat of arrest and attack by police

CELL BLOCKED
IMPRISONED FOR PEACE

Activists, presidents, prisoners: These courageous visionaries embarked on crusades for justice and equality—crusades that landed each of them behind bars. Their harrowing tales teach an important lesson: When you choose to stand up for the freedom of others, sometimes you have to sacrifice your own.

THE GREAT SOUL: Mohandas Gandhi (1869–1948)

While leading the crusade for India's independence from the British Empire in the early 1900s, Mohandas Gandhi relied on a form of protest known as civil disobedience. He had been inspired by the ideas of 19th-century American writer Henry David Thoreau, who wrote that citizens had a duty to stand up against unjust governments.

Under British rule, Indians were treated like second-class citizens and forbidden from producing their own goods. They had no say in how they were ruled until Gandhi developed a way to empower them. He rallied large groups of Indian people to block the streets, boycott British stores and courts, and refuse to work until the government had to give in. The nonviolent protests landed Gandhi in jail again and again, and each time he would refuse to eat. He was so beloved by fellow Indians—thousands joined him on a 241-mile (388-km) march to protest a tax on salt—that British authorities had to let him go before he died of starvation. Gandhi's decades of practicing civil disobedience worked. India achieved independence in 1947, and "Mahatma" Gandhi—a title meaning "great soul"—is considered by many to be the father of the nation.

FROM PRISONER TO PRESIDENT: Nelson Mandela
(1918–2013)

Nelson Mandela grew up in a nation with a deep racial divide. Blacks, Indians, Asians, and other nonwhite people in his country of South Africa were denied civil rights through a series of laws. This system of discrimination became known as apartheid in 1948. Even though they were in the minority, white people had all the power. Blacks and other nonwhites couldn't vote, and they lost all representation in government. They had limited access to education and good jobs. They couldn't travel into white neighborhoods unless they had permission, and some were even forced to live together in special "homelands." While America was making strides in civil rights in the 1960s, South Africa was sliding backward.

Nelson Mandela wanted to change that. For two decades, he organized peaceful protests, workers' strikes, and other forms of civil disobedience against apartheid in

THE SMOOTH REVOLUTIONARY:
Václav Havel (1936–2011)

Revolutions are usually violent transitions of power marred by bloody battles between the overthrowers and the overthrown. The Velvet Revolution of 1989, in what was then known as Czechoslovakia, was different. In just a few weeks of peaceful protests, without a single shot fired, the ruling Communist Party was replaced by a budding democratic government. The world was astonished by both the peaceful transition and the man who made it happen. Václav Havel, a playwright who became a political prisoner, would soon have a new job title: president.

When Czechoslovakia came under communist control in 1948, the government assumed complete authority. Secret police

would pounce on anyone who was critical of their leaders. As a young Czech with a way with words, Havel hid his criticism of the government in one-act plays that he performed in underground theaters. He helped found Charter 77, a movement that relied on the same nonviolent tactics as Gandhi. His writing and activism brought Havel leagues of young followers—and trouble from the secret police. He was jailed many times for "anti-state activities." He kept writing critical letters from jail even though it was forbidden.

But by the late 1980s, communism was crumbling across Eastern Europe, and Havel—as Czechoslovakia's most famous critic of the Communist Party—found himself leading the charge for change. He was elected as the country's first president after his Velvet Revolution in 1989. When Czechoslovakia split into the countries of Slovakia and the Czech Republic in 1993, he became the first president of the Czech Republic.

GUTSY GALS

THE NATION REBUILDER:
Ellen Johnson Sirleaf
(1938–)

In the years leading up to her election as Liberia's first female president in 2005, Ellen Johnson Sirleaf had been imprisoned and forced into exile for criticizing the African country's dictators. No one thought she could win. But the women of Liberia came out to support Sirleaf by the thousands because they believed she could bring peace to their country, which had been torn apart by 14 years of civil war as opposing groups vied to control the government.

When she took office, the nation was in shambles: The war had destroyed hospitals and caused teachers to flee, leaving a generation of children without education. There was no food or electricity, and the streets of the capital were lined with trash. But Sirleaf rose to the challenge, introducing free schooling, helping her country climb out of debt, and empowering Liberian women—which earned her the Nobel Peace Prize in 2011. In a country struggling to rebuild, Sirleaf—the first female head of state of any nation in Africa—is a symbol of hope.

the vein of Gandhi. He formed a law firm that provided free legal help to black people. When police answered the protests with violence in 1960, Mandela became disheartened and considered a more militant approach. In 1961, he was arrested and sent to prison.

Over the next two decades, as the world began turning against South Africa for its racist apartheid policies, the South African government began offering Mandela freedom from prison in exchange for him ending his opposition to the government. He always refused. After 27 years behind bars, he was finally released in 1990. He worked with South African president F. W. de Klerk to allow all races in South Africa to vote in the next election for president. When the country's first democratic elections were held in 1994, Mandela won the presidency. Apartheid had finally come to an end.

HOW TO CHANGE THE WORLD

FIVE KID-TESTED METHODS FOR MAKING A DIFFERENCE

METHOD 2: FIND A CAUSE

Some people across the country and around the world have it rough. They might lack food or opportunities or even clean drinking water. Finding these problems is often just an Internet search away, and helping to fix them isn't as hard as you think.

FOLLOW THE LEADER: RYAN HRELJAC

This Canadian kid was in first grade when he learned that people in the African country of Uganda had to walk for miles just to collect drinking water and that even then some got sick because the water wasn't clean. Young Hreljac decided to help. He raised money by doing chores and taking donations to build a well in a Ugandan village. Hreljac visited the village and made many friends there. His story became a media sensation. With help from a charity, he set up the Ryan's Well Foundation, which today builds clean-water projects across Africa and other developing countries.

METHOD 1: MAKE A NEW FRIEND

Search for chums outside your social circles: boys and girls who might not look like you, perhaps from other countries, and with different cultural backgrounds. You'd be surprised at how much you have in common. Your friendships will demolish cultural walls and make the world seem like a smaller—and friendlier—place.

FOLLOW THE LEADER: KRISHNA "DYLAN" MAHALINGAM

When he was just nine years old, this Internet whiz kid from New Hampshire, U.S.A., began making friends online with children in other parts of the world. He learned of their problems with hunger, poverty, and access to education and health care. Mahalingam tapped into a United Nations aid program called Millennium Development Goals (MDGs) to co-found a nonprofit organization called Lil' MDGs, which motivates children around the world to work together to improve their lives.

METHOD 4: START A COLLECTION

Sometimes a worthy cause needs more than just money—it needs stuff. Organize your friends and family to collect canned food for the hungry, used clothes for the homeless, school supplies for poor students, and toys for kids in need. Help your friends de-clutter their lives and you'll improve the lives of others.

FOLLOW THE LEADER: ALEX TRIESTMAN

Like most 13-year-olds, this California, U.S.A., kid loves Lego bricks. But he noticed two things about his favorite toy: They were expensive, and each set often came with extra pieces. So Triestman invented Brickshare, an organization that collects extra Lego bricks from donors. He and his friends use the pieces to build cool sets called Brickbots, which they mail to children in need around the country and the world.

METHOD 5: BECOME A ROLE MODEL

Remember back to when you were really little. What did you think of the older kids? They probably seemed smart and cool and maybe a little scary. You might even have copied them. Well, now that you're a little older, you're the one inspiring (and possibly scaring) the younger copycats. You're the Jedi knight and they're the padawans! This is your chance to be a force for good.

FOLLOW THE LEADER: DIVINE BRADLEY

Growing up in Brooklyn, New York, U.S.A., Divine Bradley noticed that kids his age and younger didn't have a safe place to socialize. When he was 17, Bradley set up a community center in his parents' basement. This hot spot quickly became too popular for its size, so Bradley founded the nonprofit organization Team Revolution, which raised more than $20,000 in just two weeks to find and fund a larger meeting space. The organization eventually offered programs teaching kids how to save money, improve their communities, and become role models like Bradley.

METHOD 3: DONATE SKILLS INSTEAD OF DOLLAR BILLS

What are your talents? Maybe you're a science whiz, or a master of social media, or great with a hammer. Once you find a cause you like, you can volunteer to use your brainpower, your time, and your muscle to help others. In the end, you might even build a business from making the world better!

FOLLOW THE LEADER: HART MAIN

This 13-year-old Ohio, U.S.A., entrepreneur got a whiff of inspiration in 2010 when he sniffed the sweet-smelling candles his sister was selling for a school fund-raiser. Why do candles have to smell so sweet? he wondered. With help from his parents, Main started Man Cans, a company that sells candles in scents like sawdust, bacon, campfire smoke, fresh-cut grass—even dirt. And instead of using traditional glass-jar candle holders, he donated soup to feed the homeless and used the empty cans for his candles. As business boomed, Main started donating money from each sale to help the homeless. His company has given 100,000 cans of soup and $35,000 to soup kitchens across four states.

CHIUNE SUGIHARA

THE DARING DIPLOMAT WHO SAVED THOUSANDS

While working at the Japanese consulate in Lithuania in 1940, Chiune Sugihara wielded a tiny tool that saved thousands of lives: a pen. That summer, Jewish refugees by the hundreds began arriving daily at the consulate where Sugihara, a Japanese diplomat, was living with his wife and children. These refugees were mostly from Poland, which had become a dangerous place for Jewish people ever since Adolf Hitler's German forces—the Nazis— had invaded it the previous year. Nazis were arresting Jewish people in Europe and sending them to work camps and prisons.

To escape the Nazis marching at their heels, Jewish refugees needed a special document—called a visa—so they could cross borders and flee Europe. Sugihara had the power to write these visas, and he asked his superiors for permission to issue them. Fearful of angering Japan's German allies in the war, they refused.

THE WRITE STUFF

Sugihara spent the night struggling with what to do. If he didn't write the visas, the refugees and their families would surely fall into the cruel hands of the Nazis. If he

> "I MAY HAVE DISOBEYED MY GOVERNMENT, BUT IF I HADN'T I WOULD HAVE BEEN DISOBEYING GOD."
> —CHIUNE SUGIHARA

FEARLESS FACTS

➔ **BORN:** January 1, 1900, Yaotsu, Japan ➔ **DIED:** July 31, 1986, Kamakura, Japan
➔ **OCCUPATION:** Diplomat at the Japanese consulate in Lithuania ➔ **BOLDEST MOMENT:** Disobeying orders and writing thousands of lifesaving visas for Jewish refugees during World War II

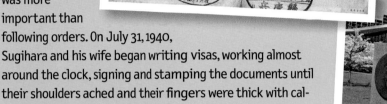

did, he risked ruining his family's future. By morning, he decided that helping people was more important than following orders. On July 31, 1940, Sugihara and his wife began writing visas, working almost around the clock, signing and stamping the documents until their shoulders ached and their fingers were thick with calluses. Each day, they produced a month's worth of visas. When the consulate closed because of the war, Sugihara moved into a hotel and kept on writing. Each visa could save not just one refugee, but his or her entire family as well.

For nearly a month they kept at it, wielding pen and stamp to produce more than 2,000 visas. When the war forced Sugihara to leave Lithuania, he threw the last few visas out the train window along with his official stamp, giving the refugees the tools they needed to create their own visas. More than 6,000 Jewish people—doctors, authors, shopkeepers, children, and elderly people—escaped Nazi-occupied Europe thanks to his efforts.

A memorial to Chiune Sugihara in Vilnius, Lithuania (below); a visa issued by Sugihara in 1940 (left)

A HERO LOST AND FOUND

Sugihara's courage cost him his career. When he returned home to Japan after the war, he was forced to resign, in part because he disobeyed orders. He never talked about his visas, but he often wondered if the documents saved any lives. In 1968, one of the surviving refugees tracked him down and began sharing his story of heroism. In 1984, on behalf of Israel, Yad Vashem declared Sugihara to be Righteous Among the Nations, an honor granted to non-Jewish people who took great risks to save Jewish people during World War II. It's estimated that as many as 40,000 people—Jewish refugees and their descendants—are alive today because Sugihara refused to obey orders.

YOUTH RESISTANCE:
Hans Scholl (1918–1943)
and Sophie Scholl (1921–1943)

Like many other Germans in the late 1930s, Hans Scholl and his sister Sophie listened to Hitler's speeches and were persuaded he was leading their country to greatness. But the Scholls' wise father, Robert, warned his children that Hitler was actually leading Germany toward destruction—and the siblings came to realize their father was right. They and a group of friends formed a small resistance group called the White Rose, which authored and distributed anti-Nazi pamphlets asking Germans to resist the regime's tyranny. On February 18, 1943, Hans and Sophie were caught leaving pamphlets at the University of Munich and were taken into custody, where they stood up for the morality of their actions in spite of the consequences it could bring. "Somebody, after all, had to make a start," Sophie was recorded as saying in court. "What we wrote and said is also believed by many others. They just do not dare express themselves as we did." Sophie, Hans, and a friend were convicted of treason and sentenced to death. The story of their bravery and humanity endures.

SOME GAVE ALL
BRINGING FORTH PROGRESS

The path to positive change is often fraught with perils. Peace activists lose their jobs, alienate friends and family, and risk insults and injury in the face of seething mobs to tell a story or stand up for what's right. These peace heroes paid a heavy price—and had a big impact on the world.

PIONEERING POLITICIAN: Harvey Milk (1930–1978)

During the early years of his life, while serving as a diver in the U.S. Navy during the Korean War and working as a public school teacher in New York, U.S.A., Harvey Milk kept a secret that he'd known about since high school: He was gay. If he let his secret slip, he risked damaging his career and becoming a target of hate. Milk's outlook changed when he moved to San Francisco in 1972 and saw his gay friends being harassed by police. He opened a camera store that became the home base of the city's growing gay community and his own campaign to enter politics. He ran for a position on the San Francisco Board of Supervisors and made powerful political connections, including San Francisco mayor George Moscone—a supporter of gay rights. In 1977, Milk finally won, becoming one of the first openly gay officials in the United States. He helped pass a city law that outlawed discrimination based on sexual orientation. Tragically, an angry former San Francisco supervisor who clashed with them politically and demanded reappointment to the Board shot and killed Milk and Moscone in 1978.

COURAGEOUS JOURNALIST: Ernie Pyle (1900–1945)

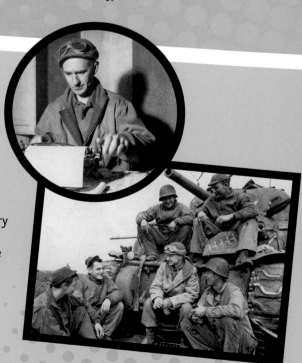

When American soldiers charged the battlefields from Africa to Okinawa in World War II, a slight, middle-aged man named Ernie Pyle followed close behind, wielding a pen and notepad instead of a rifle. As one of the first embedded journalists, Pyle lived among the troops he covered and shared their dangers. He became one of the war's most popular correspondents, famous for a reporting style that showed the terror of combat and the misery of everyday grunts mired in muddy foxholes. Pyle's stories earned him a Pulitzer Prize; his death from Japanese machine-gun fire near the end of the war brought tears to the eyes of millions of readers, the soldiers he celebrated, and First Lady Eleanor Roosevelt. The job of war correspondent is no less dangerous today. Reporters covering conflicts around the globe risk injury, kidnapping, and execution.

GRAVE INJUSTICE: Emmett Till (1941–1955)

A handsome, high-spirited teen described as hilarious to his friends and helpful to his widowed mother, Emmett Till grew up in a middle-class black neighborhood in Chicago, Illinois, U.S.A. His mother was reluctant to let Till visit relatives in Mississippi during the summer of 1955, but her only son begged to go. When she kissed him goodbye at the train station, she never saw him again. The segregated Deep South was a different world for the 14-year-old Till. When he reportedly flirted with a white clerk at a market, saying "goodbye" instead of "goodbye, ma'am," he had no idea he was risking his life. Till was kidnapped and killed by the clerk's husband and half brother a few days later. Despite overwhelming evidence of their guilt—including the courageous testimony of Till's uncle, who witnessed the kidnapping—the men were quickly acquitted of all charges by the all-white jury (black men weren't allowed to serve on juries at the time). Thousands came to Till's funeral. His horrific murder was a spark that helped ignite the civil rights movement.

BRAVE WALK FOR A CAUSE: William Lewis Moore (1927–1963)

Voted "Most Bashful" by his senior high school class, William Lewis Moore eventually overcame his shyness and tried to make the world a better place for everyone as a civil rights activist. He set out from Chattanooga, Tennessee, U.S.A., in 1963 on a 600-mile (966-km) trek to hand-deliver a letter to Ross Barnett, the segregationist governor of Mississippi, U.S.A. The letter asked the governor to accept racial integration. The long walk was no problem for this former marine turned mail carrier, who was born in the North but raised in the South, but his mission and message made him a target on the racist region's country roads. Moore wore a sign during his walk that read "Equal Rights for All, Mississippi or Bust" in bold letters. He would happily stop to discuss his cause with anyone who would listen. Tragically, about 70 miles (113 km) into his walk, Moore was shot and killed. No one was ever charged for the crime.

SHE IS NOT AFRAID: Malala Yousafzai (1997–)

GUTSY GALS

When class let out on October 9, 2012, 15-year-old Malala Yousafzai got on the bus as usual. Then something unusual—and terrifying—happened: Two strange men flagged down the bus; they boarded, and one of them pointed a pistol at her and fired. They were members of a militant group called the Taliban, which controlled Pakistan's Swat Valley, where Malala lived, ruling by fear and banning television, books, and education for women. Malala had written and shared what was happening in her town; she said that although she was afraid of the Taliban, she was determined not to let fear stop her from getting an education. Taliban leaders decided to kill her as a lesson to those who dared to stand up for freedom and education. Malala was seriously injured but miraculously survived. The attack made her a symbol for children around the world who cannot get an education. In 2014, Malala became the youngest person in history to win the Nobel Peace Prize.

DESMOND T. DOSS

HE PROTECTED AND SERVED

This shipyard worker from Virginia, U.S.A., wasn't popular with his fellow soldiers when he was drafted into the U.S. Army in 1942. They taunted him during training, and one of his officers threatened to kick him out of the military for mental illness. Doss was a conscientious objector, meaning he refused to fight because of his deeply held religious beliefs. While the soldiers around him trained for battle in World War II, Doss wouldn't even pick up a gun. He refused to work on Saturdays, the holy day in his religion. Doss's superiors came up with a workaround: They trained him to be a medic. But that didn't stop his comrades from calling him a coward.

The taunts stopped when Doss shipped off to war. During the Battle of Okinawa—the largest amphibious assault of World War II—he saved as many as 75 men who were wounded and pinned down atop a ridge. Under relentless fire from Japanese soldiers, Doss crawled to each wounded soldier, slipped him into a rope harness, and lowered him down the ridge to safety.

Later, after he was injured in a grenade attack, Doss treated his own injuries and waved off a stretcher because other wounded men needed it more. When a Japanese bullet shattered his arm weeks later, Doss finally agreed to handle a rifle—as a splint for the broken bone (the only time he ever used a weapon in combat). After the war, U.S. president Harry S. Truman presented Doss with the Congressional Medal of Honor. He was the first conscientious objector to receive the military's highest award for courage.

> "THROUGH HIS OUTSTANDING BRAVERY AND UNFLINCHING DETERMINATION IN THE FACE OF DESPERATELY DANGEROUS CONDITIONS PFC. DOSS SAVED THE LIVES OF MANY SOLDIERS." —FROM THE MEDAL OF HONOR CITATION FOR DESMOND T. DOSS

FEARLESS FACTS

➲ **BORN:** February 7, 1919, Lynchburg, Virginia, U.S.A. ➲ **DIED:** March 23, 2006, Piedmont, Alabama, U.S.A. ➲ **OCCUPATION:** U.S. Army medic ➲ **BOLDEST MOMENT:** Treating and rescuing as many as 75 fellow soldiers who were pinned down by enemy fire

JOHN LENNON

THE VOICE OF A GENERATION

It was a sing-along for the record books. In the fall of 1969, half a million protesters against the Vietnam War gathered across from the White House in Washington, D.C., U.S.A., to sing "Give Peace a Chance," an antiwar song written by a bespectacled peace activist named John Lennon. It wasn't Lennon's most famous tune. The singer-songwriter from Liverpool, England, was a founding member of the Beatles, the most successful band in music history.

The Beatles's triumph on the music charts in the 1960s brought its members more than just fame and fortune; it gave them the power to influence an entire generation of young people. When the Beatles broke up, Lennon began focusing his powers of lyrical poetry on the peace movement against the Vietnam War. Songs like "Imagine" and "Give Peace a Chance"—along with "Blowing in the Wind" by American singer-songwriter Bob Dylan—became anthems for antiwar protesters. But Lennon's influence with young people worried the administration of U.S. president Richard M. Nixon, who was up for reelection at a time when the voting age had just dropped from 21 to 18.

The Federal Bureau of Investigation (FBI) began spying on Lennon, fearful that he would stage rallies and concerts disrupting Nixon's reelection campaign. He was even ordered to leave the country. Lennon won his fight to remain in the United States but was assassinated in 1980 by a deranged fan. The world mourned.

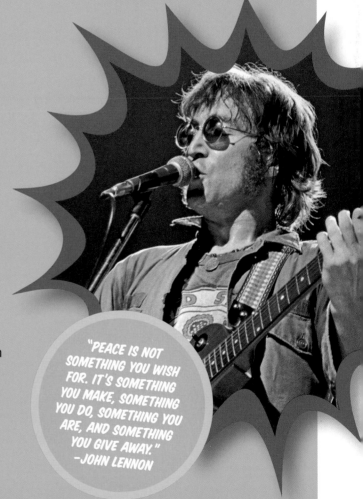

"PEACE IS NOT SOMETHING YOU WISH FOR. IT'S SOMETHING YOU MAKE, SOMETHING YOU DO, SOMETHING YOU ARE, AND SOMETHING YOU GIVE AWAY."
—JOHN LENNON

FEARLESS FACTS

➔ **BORN:** October 9, 1940, Liverpool, England ➔ **DIED:** December 8, 1980, New York, New York, U.S.A.
➔ **OCCUPATION:** Musician ➔ **BOLDEST MOMENT:** Fighting the FBI's efforts to deport him for speaking out against the Vietnam War

MOMENT OF BRAVERY

This hero faced a desperate, time-sensitive situation. How did he become the man who saved the world?

THE SITUATION

The wail of a siren shattered the early morning silence of a high-tech control center in the former Soviet Union. Computer screens flashed to life, displaying a chilling word in bold red letters: LAUNCH. The day Stanislav Petrov hoped would never come had apparently arrived; the United States had just launched a nuclear missile at his country.

Petrov was a Ukrainian officer working the night shift for the Soviet Air Defense Forces in 1983. His center, located just outside Moscow, was tapped into a network of satellites scanning for missiles from the United States, which at the time was the chief rival of the former Soviet Union. Petrov barely had time to respond to the warning when the siren sounded again. LAUNCH. LAUNCH. LAUNCH. LAUNCH. The system had detected four more missiles speeding from the other side of the world. They would reach targets in the Soviet Union in half an hour.

Petrov's orders were clear: Pick up the hotline to the military's top commanders and inform them of the missile alert. Any other action could be considered treason. He was also well aware that tensions between the Soviet Union and the United States were high; if he did his duty and reported the missile warnings, there's a good chance the officers up the chain of command would decide to launch a counterattack, initiating a global thermonuclear war that would kill millions. But it wasn't Petrov's duty to think about these things. He was only supposed to pass along the information. If America's missiles were truly inbound, the Soviet Union needed to retaliate before it was too late. And time was running out.

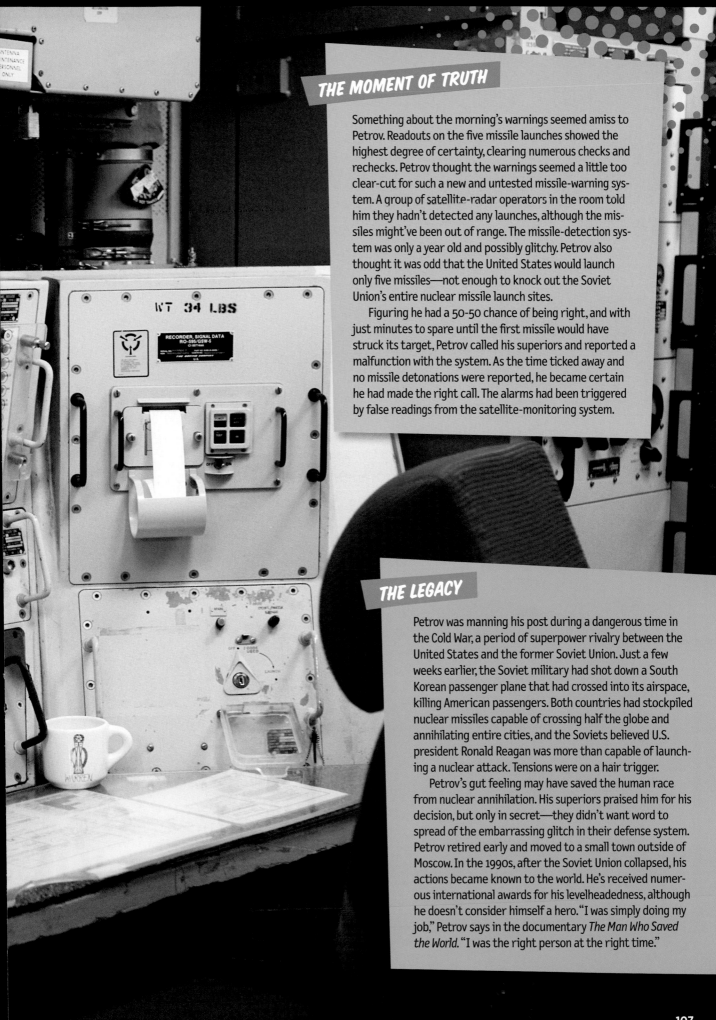

THE MOMENT OF TRUTH

Something about the morning's warnings seemed amiss to Petrov. Readouts on the five missile launches showed the highest degree of certainty, clearing numerous checks and rechecks. Petrov thought the warnings seemed a little too clear-cut for such a new and untested missile-warning system. A group of satellite-radar operators in the room told him they hadn't detected any launches, although the missiles might've been out of range. The missile-detection system was only a year old and possibly glitchy. Petrov also thought it was odd that the United States would launch only five missiles—not enough to knock out the Soviet Union's entire nuclear missile launch sites.

Figuring he had a 50-50 chance of being right, and with just minutes to spare until the first missile would have struck its target, Petrov called his superiors and reported a malfunction with the system. As the time ticked away and no missile detonations were reported, he became certain he had made the right call. The alarms had been triggered by false readings from the satellite-monitoring system.

THE LEGACY

Petrov was manning his post during a dangerous time in the Cold War, a period of superpower rivalry between the United States and the former Soviet Union. Just a few weeks earlier, the Soviet military had shot down a South Korean passenger plane that had crossed into its airspace, killing American passengers. Both countries had stockpiled nuclear missiles capable of crossing half the globe and annihilating entire cities, and the Soviets believed U.S. president Ronald Reagan was more than capable of launching a nuclear attack. Tensions were on a hair trigger.

Petrov's gut feeling may have saved the human race from nuclear annihilation. His superiors praised him for his decision, but only in secret—they didn't want word to spread of the embarrassing glitch in their defense system. Petrov retired early and moved to a small town outside of Moscow. In the 1990s, after the Soviet Union collapsed, his actions became known to the world. He's received numerous international awards for his levelheadedness, although he doesn't consider himself a hero. "I was simply doing my job," Petrov says in the documentary *The Man Who Saved the World*. "I was the right person at the right time."

CHAPTER
SIX

ACTION HEROES

Get ready to root for the good guys: real-life James Bonds and G.I. Joes, explorers who charted the uncharted and conservationists bent on saving the world. In times of war and peace, on horseback or in the air, undercover or in the thick of it, these action heroes kept their cool and demonstrated courage under fire. Blockbusters are made and best-sellers are written about the men (and women) in this chapter. Believe it or not, all these tales are true.

Harrison Ford, seen here as
Indiana Jones, is a hero both on
and off the silver screen.

ROBERT GOULD SHAW

LEADING THE CHARGE TO FREEDOM

"THE EYES OF THOUSANDS WILL LOOK ON WHAT YOU DO TONIGHT."
-ROBERT GOULD SHAW TO HIS SOLDIERS BEFORE THEIR HISTORIC CHARGE ON FORT WAGNER

After the battle in which he gave his life, Colonel Robert Gould Shaw's body was dumped into a grave along with the bodies of the men he led. His crude burial was meant as an insult by the enemy, but Shaw's father saw it differently. "We can imagine no holier place than that in which he lies," Shaw's father later wrote, "among his brave and devoted followers, nor wish for him better company." That company was an important new force in the Union Army during the American Civil War: black soldiers. Shaw was their first commander.

FORTUNATE SON

Born into a rich family in Boston, Massachusetts, U.S.A., Robert Gould Shaw was destined for a life of travel and a cushy career at his uncle's business firm. That all changed when the Civil War erupted in 1861. Fiercely patriotic, Shaw joined the Union Army of the North in its battle against the Confederacy, the southern states that broke away from the Union over the right to keep slaves. Shaw's parents

FEARLESS FACTS

➡ **BORN:** October 10, 1837, Boston, Massachusetts, U.S.A. ➡ **DIED:** July 18, 1863, Morris Island, South Carolina, U.S.A. ➡ **OCCUPATION:** Colonel in the Union Army ➡ **BOLDEST MOMENT:** Leading one of the Union Army's first black regiments in an attack on a Confederate fort during the American Civil War

were abolitionists, meaning they opposed slavery, and young Shaw grew up among many famous like-minded people. He was the natural choice to lead one of the Union Army's first black regiments.

FREEDOM FORCE

For black northerners, the Civil War was a chance to fight for the freedom of all black people in America. Massachusetts formed one of the first regiments, called the 54th Massachusetts Infantry, recruited from black northerners as well as some escaped slaves from the South. Despite the dangerous duty, the 54th Massachusetts had its full force of 1,100 volunteers by early 1863.

The 54th's first battle against a Confederate assault ended in swift victory. When Shaw was asked if his regiment would lead the attack against Fort Wagner—an important Confederate base on a South Carolina beach—he accepted the honor without hesitation. This was the 54th's chance to demonstrate the bravery and abilities of all black soldiers.

Shaw chose 600 of his men for the attack. His commanders believed the fort would be lightly defended after heavy bombardment from Union artillery. They were wrong. More than 1,700 Confederate soldiers waited inside the fort's thick walls. Just past 6:30 p.m. on July 18, 1863, Shaw led his men down a beach snarled with branches and barbed wire.

FINAL ASSAULT

The parapet (protective wall) of the fort erupted in a sheet of flame. Its defenders opened fire on the 54th with their rifles and cannons. Through the chaos of exploding artillery shells, the soldiers charged across the fort's moat and began scaling the walls. Just as he reached the top, Shaw was shot and killed. He was just 25 years old.

More than 1,500 Union soldiers—20 percent of them black members of the 54th—perished in wave after wave of follow-up attacks. Word of the regiment's bravery and abilities traveled throughout the North and South, and the sacrifice of Shaw and his soldiers is still honored today.

Colonel Robert Gould Shaw (above left); the storming of Fort Wagner (above right)

FAMOUS FIGHTERS OF THE 54TH

➔ **CHARLES AND LEWIS DOUGLASS:** These two men were the sons of Frederick Douglass, the famous abolitionist. Douglass believed that allowing black soldiers to fight in the Union Army would help all black Americans earn respect and more rights when the war was over.

➔ **WILLIAM HARVEY CARNEY:** This former slave became the first black soldier to win the Medal of Honor, the United States' highest military honor, after he grabbed the American flag from a wounded comrade and carried it through the battle, despite being shot several times. "The old flag never touched the ground!" he shouted when he returned the colors to his regiment after the harrowing battle.

➔ **JOHN WILSON:** This freedman from Cincinnati, Ohio, U.S.A., was promoted to sergeant major after the battle of Fort Wagner. He was one of only five black noncommissioned officers in the 54th (all the officers were white).

YOUNG AND FEARLESS
SEVEN COURAGEOUS KIDS

Superhero kids have emerged throughout history to rise to all kinds of challenges—sometimes they even wear a cape! These courageous kids have followed their conscience or their dream and have proved that bravery shouldn't be measured by years but by deeds.

FRIEND OF ALL FINS: Sean Lesniak
(2004–)

Like any good superhero, Sean Lesniak has a cool name for his alter ego: Shark Boy. Fascinated by the fearsome finned predators since he was three, Lesniak was horrified to learn of the barbaric practice of finning, or the removal of fins from an estimated 100 million sharks each year. Lesniak spoke before Massachusetts state legislators and helped persuade them to pass a law that banned the sale, trade, or possession of shark fins. Afterward, he joined marine biologist Greg Skomal in tagging sharks in the wild, a practice that allows scientists to study their behaviors and health.

BEATING THE ODDS: William Horsfall (1847–1922)

Children were forbidden from fighting during the American Civil War, but many ended up on the battlefield anyway. They were drummer boys, some as young as 10 years old, armed with a musical instrument instead of a rifle. In the days before radio communication, it was a drummer boy's job to signal commands using different drum beats, which could be heard over the din of battle. It was a dangerous job even for the bravest of boys, and one of the bravest among them was William Horsfall. During a battle in Corinth, Mississippi, U.S.A., in 1862, under a hail of enemy fire, Horsfall rescued a wounded officer from the battlefield. He became one of the youngest recipients of the Medal of Honor, America's highest military honor.

COMPACT CAPED CRUSADER: Miles Scott

It was a busy day—even for Batman. Speeding across the city of San Francisco, California, U.S.A., he rescued a woman tied to cable-car tracks, defused a bomb, foiled a bank robbery, and then chased the villainous Penguin to his hidden lair. Billionaire Bruce Wayne wasn't beneath the cowl of this particular Caped Crusader. Instead, Batman's alter ego was Miles Scott, a five-year-old cancer patient who dreamed of fighting crime. The Make-a-Wish Foundation made it happen, hiring actors to play bad guys and working with officials to transform San Francisco into Gotham City for one day in November 2013. While thousands of residents cheered him on, Scott sped from crime scene to crime scene in a Lamborghini Batmobile. After Scott saved the day, San Francisco's mayor awarded this brave cancer-fighting Batkid the key to the city.

SURVIVORS AT SEA: The Tokelau Teens

The three teenagers had been missing for so long that their families had held memorial services for them. Etueni Nasau, Samuel Pelesa, and Filo Filo, all cousins from the New Zealand atolls of Tokelau, had set out for a quick trip in a boat no bigger than a compact car. Then their motor sputtered and died. The cousins watched helplessly as their home island shrank over the horizon, but they never lost hope. Working together, they grabbed flying fish for food and collected rainwater from the tropical storms that tossed their tiny boat. After drifting at least 750 miles (1,207 km) in the South Pacific for more than 50 days, they spotted a fishing boat on the horizon. Rescue was at hand! They returned home—skinny but alive—to a hero's welcome.

TEENAGE TRAILBLAZER: Sacagawea (ca 1788–1812)

GUTSY GALS

This daughter of a Native American chief became the only female member of the Lewis and Clark expedition dispatched to explore the middle of the United States in the early 1800s (see pages 116–117). Although she was just 16 or 17 years old, Sacagawea possessed crucial skills for the mission. She knew which plants could serve as food and medicine, and she assured other Native American tribes that the explorers came in peace. When high winds nearly capsized one of the expedition's boats, Sacagawea calmly fished their charts and journals from the river before they could drift away, saving the mission from disaster. On the return trip through her homeland in what is now Idaho, Sacagawea led the expedition through the Shoshone trails of her childhood. Clark affectionately called her his pilot.

NATHAN HALE

AMERICA'S FIRST SPY

> "I ONLY REGRET THAT I HAVE BUT ONE LIFE TO LOSE FOR MY COUNTRY."
> —NATHAN HALE

America's battle for independence from England was not going well during the early days of the Revolutionary War. After British forces captured Long Island, New York, U.S.A., and crushed his army in August 1776, General George Washington came up with a daring mission to stay one step ahead of the enemy. He put the call out for spies to snoop on British forces. Nathan Hale, a schoolteacher turned soldier from Connecticut, U.S.A., was the sole volunteer. He was just 21 years old.

Hale's mission was dangerous to the extreme—the British Army's punishment for spying was death by hanging. Disguised as a Dutch schoolteacher, Hale sailed to Long Island and blended with the locals. Under the noses of England's redcoat soldiers, he drew maps of their fortifications and began tracking enemy troop movements. Hale wrote notes in Latin and hid them in his shoes. But his luck soon ran out. Accounts of his capture vary, but America's first spy fell into British hands on September 21, 1776. Hale's captors found his hidden notes. The redcoats had caught him red-handed.

Hale's finest hours would be his last. The British gave their captive the opportunity to switch sides and become a double agent, spying on the Americans. Hale refused. Without a trial or opportunity to defend himself, he was quickly sentenced to death by hanging and led to the gallows on September 22. It was here that his legend was born. According to the few witnesses to his execution, Hale calmly walked to the noose with dignity. His final words echo through history: "I only regret that I have but one life to lose for my country."

FEARLESS FACTS

→ **BORN:** June 6, 1755, Coventry, Connecticut, U.S.A. → **DIED:** September 22, 1776, New York, New York, U.S.A. → **OCCUPATION:** Schoolteacher, soldier in the Continental Army → **BOLDEST MOMENT:** Bidding a bold goodbye as he was about to be executed for spying

WITOLD PILECKI

THE SPY WHO BROKE INTO PRISON

The Nazis grabbed Witold Pilecki off the streets of Warsaw, Poland, and sent him to a prison called Auschwitz. Once there, he was stripped of his belongings and assigned backbreaking work. Everything was going according to his plan.

Pilecki was a spy for the Polish resistance movement, which he helped form in 1939 after Germany invaded Poland at the start of World War II. His mission: to infiltrate Auschwitz. Prisoners who entered this work camp often never came out, and Pilecki wanted to find out why. So he allowed himself to be caught by the Nazis in 1940, as they were rounding up thousands of civilians.

His worst fears about Auschwitz were soon realized. Prisoners were forced to perform heavy labor in the freezing cold. Many were put to death in chambers of poisonous gas, and those who didn't perish in the chambers died of starvation or disease or medical experiments. More than a million people were killed there.

Dodging lethal labor and the gas chamber, Pilecki stuck to his mission for nearly two and a half years. He recruited other prisoners into a spy ring and plotted against his captors. The spies sneaked out messages with escapees and laundry workers. They even built a secret radio transmitter and broadcast messages to the Polish resistance. Because of Pilecki's courage, the outside world learned of the horrors of Auschwitz, one of the Nazis' infamous concentration camps. His mission complete, Pilecki escaped. He rejoined the resistance and continued to fight the Germans until the end of the war.

> "A MAN FIGHTING FOR HIS LIFE CAN DO MORE THAN HE EVER IMAGINED HE COULD."
> —WITOLD PILECKI

FEARLESS FACTS

→ **BORN:** May 13, 1901, Olonets, Karelia, Russia → **DIED:** May 25, 1948, Warsaw, Poland
→ **OCCUPATION:** Soldier, spy → **BOLDEST MOMENT:** Infiltrating a Nazi concentration camp during World War II

GOING THE DISTANCE
EXTRAORDINARY EXPLORERS

How far would you go to make a great discovery? How much would you risk to prove the impossible is indeed possible? These bold adventurers ventured into uncharted territory and soared to new heights. In the process, they made their mark on history and filled in the gaps on our maps.

FIRST IN TRANSATLANTIC FLIGHT:
Charles Lindbergh (1902–1974)

Airplane technology wasn't even a quarter of a century old in 1927, and soaring over vast stretches of empty ocean was risky in the days before satellite navigation. Daredevil pilot Charles Lindbergh was eager to make the first nonstop transatlantic flight all by himself. In May 1927, he took off from an airfield on Long Island, New York, U.S.A., in a plane called the *Spirit of St. Louis.* He flew through complete darkness, skimming the waves near Ireland to make sure he was still on course. Nearly 34 hours later, he landed at an airfield near Paris, France, where more than 100,000 people watched his historic landing. Lindbergh's flight set the stage for modern long-distance air travel. A flight from New York to Paris today takes less than eight hours.

CHARTING THE UNCHARTED: Lewis and Clark
(1774–1809) and (1770–1838)

It was an important mission—one directly from the president. In 1803, the relatively new United States of America had just doubled its size with the Louisiana Purchase, a sprawling stretch of the continent extending west of the Mississippi River. President Thomas Jefferson believed the new land would be filled with wonders, from woolly mammoths to towering volcanoes, so he dispatched his secretary Captain Meriwether Lewis and his friend William Clark on an expedition to see what was out there.
Leading an expedition of more than 30 rugged outdoorsmen (and one teenage girl, Native American guide Sacagawea), Lewis and Clark embarked on their 8,000-mile (12,800-km) mission in 1804, using poles

Christopher Columbus sailed into the history books when he landed in the New World (the Americas) in 1492, but archaeologists now think the history books got it wrong. Five hundred years before Columbus set sail, a Viking explorer named Leif Eriksson voyaged from Greenland to "Vinland," now believed to be the northern tip of Newfoundland, Canada.

Born in Norway, Eriksson grew up in the shadow of his famous father, Erik the Red, who established the first European settlement in Greenland. Explorer's blood coursed through Eriksson's veins; seamanship came naturally to him. Sometime around the year 1000, he boarded a small longboat with a crew of 35 men and sailed to North America. Historians aren't certain of the circumstances surrounding his journey. Eriksson possibly landed by mistake after being blown off course, or he may have been following a tip from a fellow Viking who claimed he spotted a mysterious landmass. Regardless, Eriksson was the first European to set foot on the continent. (Archaeologists in 1960 believed they found evidence of his camp.) He spent just one winter in Vinland before sailing home.

HER DEEPNESS: Sylvia Earle (1935–) GUTSY GALS

When Sylvia Earle was in graduate school studying marine biology, she applied for a position as a teaching assistant. Even though she was the best qualified applicant, she didn't get the job. "They said, 'It has to go to a man, because a woman will just get married and have babies,'" she remembers. They probably regret passing her over now. For the past five decades, Earle has clocked more than 7,000 hours exploring the deep oceans. She's discovered thousands of species, led more than 50 expeditions, and set a record for the lowest depth a human has explored on foot when she took a stroll 1,250 feet (381 m) below the surface of the Pacific Ocean. In 2009, she started a foundation called Mission Blue, which aims to create protected areas of the ocean— similar to what national parks do on land. Earle has won countless awards for her work and earned the nickname Her Deepness.

to push their barge along the Missouri River. They carried everything they would need for an expedition in the wilds, including rifles, warm clothes, food in case the hunting became hard, and trinkets to trade with the Native Americans. Instead of woolly mammoths and volcanoes, they encountered grizzly bears and the treacherous Rocky Mountains, mosquito swarms, and extreme weather. They reached the Pacific Ocean a year later, then they headed home. Only one member of their expedition died—of a burst appendix— on their daring mission to map the unmapped.

REEL HEROES

FIVE MOVIE STARS WHO *SAVED* THE DAY *OFF* THE SET

PAUL ROBESON (1898–1976)

IN THE MOVIES: He might be the most famous movie star you never heard of. In the 1920s and '30s, this former lawyer starred in a variety of movies and musicals—at a time when black actors were rare. Robeson was also an accomplished stage actor and singer.

IN REAL LIFE: Robeson was an advocate for social justice across the world and could speak more than 20 languages. He used his celebrity to call attention to the poor treatment of black Americans—particularly the segregation and violence against minorities in the American South. This made him unpopular in Hollywood and cost him many big roles. Frustrated with the way movies portrayed black people, he quit acting in 1942 and focused on his fight for civil rights.

HARRISON FORD (1942–)

IN THE MOVIES: Ford whips evildoers as Indiana Jones and flies the *Millennium Falcon* as the rogue smuggler Han Solo in the *Star Wars* films.

IN REAL LIFE: He owns his own helicopter and offers to fly it—free of charge—for search-and-rescue missions near his ranch in Jackson, Wyoming, U.S.A. In 2000, he touched down in a meadow halfway up a mountain to rescue a woman who had become sick during her climb. Instead of Chewbacca at his side, Ford flew with a paramedic, who treated the hiker during the flight to the hospital. The woman didn't realize Indiana Jones was in the cockpit until after she lost her lunch in the paramedic's hat. "I can't believe I barfed in Harrison Ford's helicopter," she later said. The following summer, Ford swooped to the rescue again when he found a 13-year-old Boy Scout named Cody Clawson lost in Yellowstone National Park. "I was like, 'Oh God, Han Solo just rescued me!'" Clawson later told the press. "How cool is that?"

JIMMY STEWART (1908–1997)

IN THE MOVIES: One of Hollywood's most beloved actors, Stewart played charming dudes in dozens of classic movies, from the holiday classic *It's a Wonderful Life* to the romantic comedy *The Philadelphia Story*.

IN REAL LIFE: When the United States entered World War II in 1941, Stewart put his acting career on hold and enlisted as a pilot in the Army Air Corps (which would eventually become the Air Force). Stewart was the first big movie star to serve in the war, and his superiors were reluctant to send a celebrity into battle. After pushing for combat duty, Stewart flew more than 20 combat missions as a bomber pilot and rose to the rank of colonel by the war's end. He returned home with numerous medals for bravery and resumed his acting career.

JACKIE CHAN (1954–)

IN THE MOVIES: This ultimate action hero (you may recognize him as Mr. Han from the recent *Karate Kid* movies) is famous for doing all of his own stunts—from bone-crunching martial arts fights to flinging himself off zooming trucks. Many of his blockbusters are funny as well as thrilling, even if outtakes during the ending credits make audiences wince at stunts gone wrong. Chan has been rushed to the hospital many times for too many injuries to list.

IN REAL LIFE: Chan is generous with the money he makes from his movies. He has donated to hundreds of charities and set up his own charitable foundations for poor children and elderly people in China, his home country. He also campaigns for endangered animals and helps raise funds for disaster relief. He may have fractured his skull, lost teeth, damaged his spine, and broken his breastbone in his movies, but Chan's heart is still in the right place.

CHRISTOPHER REEVE (1952–2004)

IN THE MOVIES: As Superman, sole survivor of the doomed planet Krypton, Reeve soared faster than a speeding bullet in a red-and-blue suit and saved the Earth in sequel after sequel.

IN REAL LIFE: An avid horseback rider, Reeve was thrown from the saddle during a 1995 riding show. He broke his neck in the fall and became paralyzed from the neck down. Reeve was confined to an electric wheelchair, but he never gave up hope that he would walk again. Until his death, in 2004, he shared that hope with other victims of similar injuries. With his wife, he formed the Christopher and Dana Reeve Foundation to fund cures for spinal cord injuries and improve the quality of life for people living with paralysis.

SPARTACUS

FROM CHAINS TO CHAMPION

Gladiators were the pro athletes of ancient Rome. For more than 600 years, spectators filled arenas across the Roman Republic (which later became the Roman Empire) to watch these highly trained warriors do battle. But although they were celebrities, most gladiators were slaves or prisoners of war forced into fighting for the bloodthirsty crowd's amusement. One gladiator turned the tables on his Roman captors and led a famous slave revolt that erupted into an all-out war. His name was Spartacus, the most famous gladiator who ever lived.

SPARTACUS FOUGHT AGAINST INJUSTICE AND FACED IMPOSSIBLE ODDS.

FEARLESS FACTS

➲ **BORN:** 111 B.C., Thracia (modern-day Bulgaria) ➲ **DIED:** 71 B.C., near Petelia (modern-day Italy)
➲ **OCCUPATION:** Gladiator ➲ **BOLDEST MOMENT:** Leading an uprising of fellow slaves and fighting their way to freedom

ARENA HERO

Much of Spartacus's early life is a mystery. Historians believe he was a soldier from Thracia, a province of the Roman Republic, and he was sold into slavery for reasons unknown. Like many soldiers turned slaves, Spartacus was sent to a gladiator school to master the wielding of weapons. Because he was a special heavyweight gladiator, Spartacus focused on using a shield and a short sword with a nasty edge. He also trained in other weapons: short spears for stabbing, long spears for keeping gladiators on horseback at bay, and exotic tools such as nets that tangled opponents.

Like his fellow gladiators, Spartacus was forced to take part in gory spectacles. He waged bloody one-on-one fights with other warriors, took part in reenactments of famous battles, and engaged in live hunts for exotic animals. Although gladiators rarely fought to the death, it was still a dangerous job fraught with injuries. By 73 B.C., Spartacus had had enough.

A color engraving of Spartacus

Eventually, officials in Rome had become terrified of Spartacus's seemingly unstoppable success. They assembled 50,000 soldiers and all but declared war on the gladiator general, finally defeating his forces in 71 B.C. They assumed Spartacus fell in battle, although his body was never found. His name lives on as an inspiration for oppressed people fighting against injustice and impossible odds.

FIGHT TO THE FINISH

He plotted an escape with 70 fellow gladiators at his school. Using kitchen utensils as weapons, they battled their way to the armory, where they equipped themselves with real weapons and shields. Now properly armed as well as dangerous, the escapees fled to Mount Vesuvius, a volcano near the city of Pompeii. Leading his small army of gladiators, Spartacus defeated thousands of Roman soldiers sent to recapture him. His victories inspired slaves from across ancient Rome. They escaped from their owners to join his army, which swelled to more than 60,000. Spartacus had gone from gladiator to general.

Spartacus's army wasn't the first slave uprising in the Roman Republic (it became known as the Third Servile War), but it was the largest and most threatening to the powers that be.

MORE SUCCESSFUL THAN SPARTACUS: Toussaint L'Ouverture

Born a slave in 1743 in the French Caribbean colony of St. Dominique, Toussaint L'Ouverture spent his childhood learning to read, studying history, and mastering languages (he spoke three by the time he was 20). The brilliant L'Ouverture had earned his own freedom by 1791, when other slaves in the colony began fighting back against their brutal treatment on the sugarcane plantations. Although he could have stayed out of the fight, L'Ouverture decided to join it. A brilliant military strategist, he became the leader of not only history's largest slave revolt, but its most successful. His leadership transformed St. Dominique into the island nation of Haiti. Today he is considered one of its founding fathers.

WORLD WARRIORS
FIVE EARTH DEFENDERS

Wherever the planet was under attack—from ocean pollution, overhunting of endangered animals, or rain forest deforestation—these adventurous souls fought back. Without their passion and pluck, we wouldn't have national parks, protected species, or an appreciation for the creatures of land and sea. Meet some of Mother Nature's most daring defenders ...

CONSERVATIONIST IN CHIEF:
Theodore Roosevelt (1858–1919)

The youngest president in U.S. history (he was just 42 when he took office in 1901), Theodore "Teddy" Roosevelt was more of an action hero than a politician. Prior to his presidency, Roosevelt had been a cowboy, a soldier who led the Rough Riders cavalry into battle in the Spanish-American War, a New York City police commissioner, and a big-game hunter. But through it all he maintained a passion for the great outdoors. He even liked to rough it as president, camping with famous naturalist John Muir in Yosemite National Park. While in office, Roosevelt used his power to protect his passion. He set aside pristine tracts of American wilderness to create 150 national forests, five national parks, and many bird sanctuaries and game reserves—roughly 230 million total acres (93 million ha) of protected public land. He also created the U.S. Forest Service to look after it all.

SEA BELIEVER: Jacques Cousteau (1910–1997)

If it has gills, scales, fins, or tentacles, then it probably appeared in Jacques Cousteau's television shows and books, which introduced viewers above the ocean's surface to the mysterious world below it. Born in France in 1910, Cousteau grew fascinated with the sea in the 1920s after taking up swimming to recover from a car accident. Underwater exploration and photography gear didn't exist yet, so Cousteau helped invent it, testing the equipment himself. (This brave explorer was also a spy for the French Resistance during World War II.) Aboard the *Calypso*, an old British Royal Navy vessel he purchased in 1950, Cousteau traveled the world's oceans with his family and film crew in tow, producing more than 120 television documentaries. He also became one of the world's first conservationists. Before his death in 1997, Cousteau worked tirelessly to fight ocean pollution, overfishing, and commercial whaling.

WILDLIFE KNIGHT: Steve Irwin (1962–2006)

The world's deadliest animals had a best buddy in Australian conservationist Steve Irwin. Snakes, spiders, sharks, and especially crocodiles got the star treatment on his television show *The Crocodile Hunter*, on which the energetic host got up close and personal with supposedly dangerous creatures to show us we had little to fear. Unfortunately, Irwin died in 2006 in a freak accident while swimming with a stingray. But his enthusiasm and conservation work live on in his Wildlife Warriors foundation, which protects threatened and endangered wildlife. Irwin's daughter, Bindi, is following in her father's footsteps, hosting shows that demonstrate we have nothing to fear from scary animals.

FOREST GUARDIAN: René Ngongo (1961–)

A source of lifesaving medicines, home to roughly half of Earth's plant and animal species, a filter for planet-heating greenhouses gases—the benefits of the world's rain forests go on and on. Unfortunately, so do these forests' threats, which include illegal logging and cutting down the trees for fuel and farmland. Defending these essential forests is a dangerous job. Dozens of conservationists in the South American Amazon—the world's largest rain forest—have been assassinated.

In the African Congo, the world's second largest rain forest, biologist René Ngongo is protecting the trees despite the risks. In 1994, he founded a nationwide organization of volunteers to monitor the rain forests—and kept it going during a six-year civil war. He exposed logging and mining companies that are clearing the forests illegally. And he has taught communities how to replant trees and grow crops without cutting them down. A native of the Congo, Ngongo has made it his mission to prove these forests are more valuable alive than cleared away.

GUTSY GALS

GORILLA GIRL: Dian Fossey (1932–1985)

In 1963, 31-year-old Dian Fossey spent her life savings on a journey to Africa. She wanted to see a creature she had only read about: the rare mountain gorilla. Like British primatologist Jane Goodall, Fossey wanted to join primate society. She groomed herself, walked on her knuckles, and imitated gorilla calls. It worked: In 1970, one of the gorillas reached out and touched her hand. Over the years Fossey began to focus her attention on preventing the poaching of gorillas and was a vocal and active advocate for their safety. In 1985, Fossey was found dead in her cabin; most people think a poacher killed her. Fossey's death was tragic, but her life brought attention to the plight of mountain gorillas, which are a protected species today.

JOHN R. FOX

THE BUFFALO SOLDIER WHO SAVED THE DAY

Dressed as civilians, German soldiers sneaked into the Italian village of Sommocolonia on Christmas night 1944. They attacked the following morning, and American troops trying to hold the town were forced into a desperate retreat. Lieutenant John R. Fox, however, volunteered to stay behind with a small team of Italian soldiers to give his fellow Americans time to escape and regroup. He settled in on the second floor of a building where he could get a better view of the enemy's position.

Fox was a member of the 92nd Infantry Division—also known as the Buffalo Soldiers. In a time when the U.S. military was still segregated, or divided by color, the 92nd was made up of black soldiers from all over the United States. It was the only black division to see combat in Europe during World War II.

As Fox and his small team watched the Germans advance, he began calling in artillery attacks. The exploding shells were slowing the Germans but not stopping them. As they continued their advance on his position, Fox called in more strikes. But the Germans kept coming. If Fox didn't stop them now, the enemy would overrun the American retreat. He had one option left. Fox ordered an artillery strike directly on his position. The artillery operator couldn't believe what he was hearing. He told Fox that the shells would destroy his building. Fox's reply was short: "Fire it!"

When they retook Sommocolonia from the Germans, the American soldiers found Fox's body among the enemy dead. His bravery and sacrifice had given his comrades time to escape and stage a successful counterattack.

"HIS EXTRAORDINARY VALOROUS ACTIONS WERE IN KEEPING WITH THE MOST CHERISHED TRADITIONS OF MILITARY SERVICE." —FROM JOHN R. FOX'S MEDAL OF HONOR CITATION

FEARLESS FACTS

◆ **BORN:** May 18, 1915, Cincinnati, Ohio, U.S.A. ◆ **DIED:** December 26, 1944, Sommocolonia, Italy
◆ **OCCUPATION:** U.S. Army officer ◆ **BOLDEST MOMENT:** Calling artillery strikes on his own position to cover his comrades' retreat

JACK CHURCHILL

While his comrades-in-arms charged into battle wielding machine guns, he slung a medieval longbow across his back and wore a fearsome Scottish sword at his waist. Englishman John Malcolm Thorpe Fleming Churchill was not only one of the bravest soldiers of World War II, he was probably the most interesting. His nickname, well-earned, was Mad Jack.

Raised in Surrey, England, Churchill sought adventure from an early age. He was an actor, a model, and an archery champion. After World War II began, he became the only British soldier to dispatch a German enemy with an arrow. Churchill thrived on the battlefield, where he was known to stalk calmly through enemy fire and shrug off injuries. He volunteered for the Commandos, a British special forces unit assigned to only the most dangerous missions.

When he led a raid on a German-occupied seaside town in Norway, he stormed the beach with bagpipes under his arm, playing an inspiring tune to embolden his men. In 1943, with the help of a corporal, Churchill sneaked into an Italian town and captured 42 German soldiers using only his sword. He was later captured by the enemy but escaped twice.

Despite his preference for weapons made for the Middle Ages rather than modern battlefields, Churchill survived the war and retired from the British military in 1959. He became an avid surfer in his later years and made a hobby out of restoring steamboats. After his death at the age of 89, the Royal Norwegian Explorers Club named him one of the finest adventurers of all time.

"ANY OFFICER WHO GOES INTO ACTION WITHOUT HIS SWORD IS IMPROPERLY DRESSED."
—LIEUTENANT COLONEL JOHN MALCOLM THORPE FLEMING "MAD JACK" CHURCHILL

FEARLESS FACTS

➔ **BORN:** September 16, 1906, Surrey, England ➔ **DIED:** March 8, 1996, Surrey, England
➔ **OCCUPATION:** British Commando ➔ **BOLDEST MOMENT:** Capturing more than 40 enemy soldiers while wielding a sword

MOMENT OF BRAVERY

The World War II ace faced a difficult decision: Obey his orders or obey his conscience. What did he choose?

THE SITUATION

Pushing the throttle of his fighter plane to the max, Lt. Franz Stigler lined up the enemy bomber in his sights. It was December 1943, the thick of World War II, and the bomber had just destroyed one of Germany's factories. Stigler, a dashing ace in the Luftwaffe (or German Air Force), put his finger on the trigger. His heart raced with excitement. He had the perfect shot!

Then Stigler noticed something peculiar. The enemy bomber's tail gunner wasn't shooting back, even though Stigler's plane was in range. In fact, the bomber didn't have a tail gun at all—it had been blasted away. As he pulled alongside the enemy plane, Stigler noticed enormous gouges in its metal skin. Sections of the tail had been obliterated. The nose was shattered. Through bullet holes in the hull, he watched desperate crew members helping their injured comrades. Only one of the three engines was still working. Clearly this bomber had taken a beating from guns and fighters defending the factory. Stigler could hardly believe it was still flying!

He locked eyes with the pilot in the bomber's cockpit, who stared back with a strange expression. Confusion, maybe? Fear? Stigler's orders were clear: Shoot down this plane. If it escaped back to its base, the crew would survive to bomb Germany another day. Disobeying those orders could land Stigler in trouble with his superiors. The decision seemed clear ... or was it?

THE MOMENT OF TRUTH

Despite his orders, Stigler chose to let the stricken bomber escape. He believed in a code shared by military pilots since airborne combat was invented in World War I: Treat your enemy with honor. Don't shoot down pilots who have parachuted to safety or are no longer in the fight. He couldn't bring himself to blast the badly damaged American bomber from the sky. Doing so would doom all the men aboard. He wouldn't be able to live with himself if he survived the war.

Stigler pulled his plane into formation with the bomber to protect it from the German guns lining the coast below. He didn't think the bomber could reach the safety of its base in England, so he began gesturing to the pilot, an American named Charlie Brown. Stigler pointed in the direction of Switzerland, a neutral country where Brown could land his crippled bomber for repairs. Brown couldn't believe what he was seeing. He thought the German plane was toying with him, preparing to blow him from the sky. He ordered a gunner in the top turret to shoot at the German plane. Stigler saw the guns swivel in his direction. He knew there was nothing else he could do. He saluted the bomber and peeled off, hoping it would find its way to safety.

THE LEGACY

Against all odds, the blasted bomber limped back to base. Fearing he would be executed for sparing the enemy bomber, Stigler never told his superiors about what happened. Both Stigler and Brown continued to fight in the war on opposite sides. They survived, but they thought of each other often—even decades after the war. Finally, in 1986, Brown decided to track down the mysterious German pilot who had spared his plane.

He scoured war records for any clues about the pilot's identity and wrote a letter for a fighter pilot newsletter. In 1990, he received a reply from Stigler, who was living in Canada. When the two finally met, they hugged and cried and became close. They traveled the country together, spreading their message that enemies can be friends. The two men were like brothers until they both died within a few months of each other in 2008.

CHAPTER SEVEN

INSPIRING MINDS

If you think the words "science" and "heroes" are a strange combination, consider this: Without scientists, we wouldn't have a cure for smallpox, a disease that claimed more than 300 million lives in the 20th century. We wouldn't have artificial hearts or video game consoles, smartphones or microwave ovens. We'd still be living in a literal dark age, without electric light to illuminate the night or the Internet to brighten our brains. Scientists save lives, or they improve them, and sometimes they sacrifice their own. Turn the page to celebrate some of the bravest brains in history.

Inventor Nikola Tesla studies electricity in his laboratory in 1900.

GALILEO GALILEI

THE FEARLESS FATHER OF ASTRONOMY

Today we take it for granted that the sun—not the Earth—sits at the center of the solar system. No one would call you weird for saying the moon is pocked with craters or that the sun has spots. When Galileo Galilei was born in 1564, these ideas weren't just crazy—they were dangerous! But Galileo saw these truths with his own eyes. Then he wrote about them, and it nearly cost him his life.

BRAVE NEW WORLDS

Albert Einstein considered Galileo the father of modern science. But in late 16th-century Italy, he was just a math teacher. To help pay his bills, Galileo wrote books about his discoveries and invented a more powerful type of telescope for merchants to scan the horizon for incoming ships. When Galileo turned his invention on the night skies, he made some startling discoveries. Jupiter was orbited by its own set of moons. Venus had phases, proving that it orbited the sun and not Earth. These discoveries were about to land Galileo in hot water with the Roman Catholic Church.

"IN QUESTIONS OF SCIENCE, THE AUTHORITY OF A THOUSAND IS NOT WORTH THE HUMBLE REASONING OF A SINGLE INDIVIDUAL."
–GALILEO GALILEI

FEARLESS FACTS

➲ **BORN:** February 15, 1564, Pisa, Italy ➲ **DIED:** January 8, 1642, Arcetri, Italy
➲ **OCCUPATION:** Teacher, scholar, astronomer ➲ **BOLDEST MOMENT:** Putting the Earth in its place and contradicting the Roman Catholic Church

The church held sacred the teachings of Greek philosopher Aristotle from nearly 2,000 years before Galileo's time. Aristotle said that heavenly bodies such as the moon and the sun were perfect spheres, free from blemishes. More importantly, all the planets, moons, and stars in the heavens were supposed to orbit the Earth, which sat motionless at the center of all creation. In 1543, Polish mathematician Nicolaus Copernicus had figured out that the Earth and its fellow planets actually orbit the sun, but—fearful of contradicting the Roman Catholic Church—didn't publish his big idea until his final days. The more Galileo studied the night sky, the more he saw that Copernicus was right and the church was wrong.

Galileo talking to skeptics about the moon

INCONVENIENT TRUTHS

But stating these beliefs was dangerous in the time of the Roman Inquisition, when church officials tortured and even killed people who spoke against the church doctrine. Imagine Galileo's frustration at seeing the truth through his telescope but not being able to share his discoveries! Eventually, he decided that scientific facts didn't necessarily contradict holy Scripture. Unfortunately for Galileo, church leaders didn't see things that way.

When Galileo published a book that supported Copernicus's point of view, he was summoned to Rome. Inquisition officials threatened Galileo with torture until he took back his claim that the Earth revolves around the sun. Charged with heresy—the crime of teaching against the church's beliefs—he was put under house arrest and forbidden from publishing any more books. But Galileo defied the church's sentence and continued to experiment and write until his death. The professor from Pisa never stopped teaching. Eventually, as scientific evidence mounted, the Roman Catholic Church could no longer argue against Galileo's observations. The church lifted its ban on Galileo's works in 1718.

GALILEO'S GIFTS TO SCIENCE

➔ **THE SCIENTIFIC METHOD:** Galileo pioneered the process of testing scientific theories through observations and experiments.

➔ **JUPITER'S MOONS:** Peering through his telescope, the most powerful of its day, Galileo discovered four of Jupiter's many moons. Later astronomers would name them the Galilean Satellites.

➔ **LAWS OF MOTION:** Galileo's experiments with swinging pendulums and balls dropped from the leaning tower of his hometown, Pisa, established the basics of modern physics.

laws of motion

the scientific method

Jupiter's moons

SCIENCE STARS
FIVE GREAT GEEKS

THE GAME BOY: Shigeru Miyamoto
(1952–)

Growing up without TV or video games in rural Japan, young Shigeru Miyamoto relied on his hyperactive imagination for entertainment. He explored the countryside, collecting bugs and pretending he was a brave adventurer surrounded by strange creatures. These adventures came to virtual life when he became an artist and game designer at Nintendo in the late 1970s. Donkey Kong, Super Mario Bros., The Legend of Zelda, Super Mario Kart—all of these landmark titles are Miyamoto's masterpieces. He's been called the Steven Spielberg of video games for a reason: His creations combine crowd-pleasing thrills and charming characters with deep, secret-filled game play.

THE MAD SCIENTIST: Nikola Tesla (1856–1943)

He's been called the greatest geek who ever lived, a real-life mad genius who helped power the world back when people relied on candles and gas lamps to light the night. Nikola Tesla was instrumental in inventing alternating current, the technology that carries electricity from power plants all the way to the outlet charging your smartphone. Born in modern-day Croatia, he moved to New York City in 1884 to work for Thomas Edison, inventor of the first commercially successful lightbulb. Edison is occasionally cast as the villain in Tesla's legend—as the man who reaped the rewards while Tesla ended up penniless and unsung. Today, Tesla's brilliance is finally getting the recognition it deserves. Along with alternating current, he helped invent the radio, x-rays, wireless power, and robots. "It will soon be possible to transmit wireless messages around the world so simply that any individual can carry and operate his own apparatus," Tesla wrote more than 70 years before the invention of the cell phone.

THE FACE OF SPACE:
Neil deGrasse Tyson (1958–)

As a teenager growing up in the Bronx in New York City, Neil deGrasse Tyson studied the night sky from his apartment building's rooftop, first with a weak pair of opera glasses and then with a more powerful telescope he bought with money saved from walking dogs. When suspicious neighbors called the police during one of Tyson's stargazing sessions, he befriended the officers by letting them peer through his telescope. He's been sharing his passion for the universe ever since. An astrophysicist with a knack for explaining the mind-boggling clockwork of the universe (a talent Tyson shares with one of his childhood heroes, astronomer Carl Sagan), Tyson is the director of the Hayden Planetarium at the American Museum of Natural History in New York City and a popular TV host. His passion has inspired the next generation of stargazers.

THE SCIENCE GUY: Bill Nye (1955–)

"Science rules!" exclaimed host Bill Nye during the theme song of his television show *Bill Nye the Science Guy,* which inspired a generation of kid scientists-in-training during its 100-episode run in the 1990s. Wearing a lab coat and his trademark bow tie, Nye taught complex scientific topics—from ocean tides to brain chemistry—by entertaining audiences with silly skits and funny songs. When he's not on TV, Nye works as a scientist and inventor. (He helped devise a small sundial for the Mars-roving robots.) Still wearing his trademark bow tie, Nye appears regularly on TV to challenge skeptics of evolution and climate change, motivating viewers to stand up for science.

PHYSICS PIONEER: Shirley Ann Jackson (1946–)

GUTSY GALS

As a kid, Shirley Ann Jackson used to crawl under her front porch to study honeybees. She followed her love of science to the Massachusetts Institute of Technology (MIT), in Cambridge, Massachusetts, U.S.A., where she became the first African-American woman to attend the prestigious university. MIT wasn't quite ready for her yet: She faced discrimination by staff and students, some of whom even refused to sit next to her. But Jackson kept her focus and, when she wasn't working, volunteered in the children's ward of a local hospital to put her troubles in perspective. In 1973, Jackson became the first black woman to earn a PhD, in physics, from MIT. She had studied subatomic particles, the building blocks of atoms; her work led to inventions such as the touch-tone telephone, solar cells, and caller ID.

ALBERT EINSTEIN

A MAN AHEAD OF HIS TIME (AND SPACE)

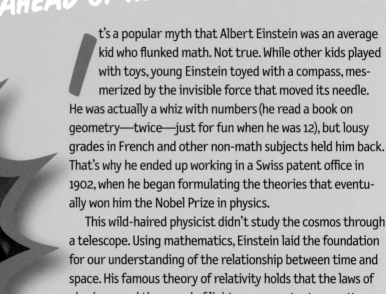

"I HAVE NO SPECIAL TALENTS. I AM ONLY PASSIONATELY CURIOUS."
–ALBERT EINSTEIN

It's a popular myth that Albert Einstein was an average kid who flunked math. Not true. While other kids played with toys, young Einstein toyed with a compass, mesmerized by the invisible force that moved its needle. He was actually a whiz with numbers (he read a book on geometry—twice—just for fun when he was 12), but lousy grades in French and other non-math subjects held him back. That's why he ended up working in a Swiss patent office in 1902, when he began formulating the theories that eventually won him the Nobel Prize in physics.

This wild-haired physicist didn't study the cosmos through a telescope. Using mathematics, Einstein laid the foundation for our understanding of the relationship between time and space. His famous theory of relativity holds that the laws of physics—and the speed of light—are constant no matter your location and motion in the universe. Space and time are not only intertwined, they become distorted when they are near a source of strong gravity (such as a black hole). This curving of space time, Einstein theorized, can lead to all sorts of wild effects, including time travel. Most of his theories have been proven correct by modern experiments and observations of space.

Also concerned with human rights issues, later in his life Einstein campaigned for the rights of black Americans and strove to make the world safer from the atomic bomb—a devastating weapon he had urged the president of the United States to build before having a change of heart. Einstein considered that advice one of his life's greatest mistakes.

FEARLESS FACTS

→ **BORN:** March 14, 1879, Ulm, Germany → **DIED:** April 18, 1955, Princeton, New Jersey, U.S.A.
→ **OCCUPATION:** Physicist → **BOLDEST MOMENT:** Brainstorming the mind-blowing general theory of relativity

CHARLES DARWIN

This self-taught English naturalist was just 22 years old when he boarded the sailing ship H.M.S. *Beagle* for what was supposed to be a two-year voyage along the coast of South America. The trip ended up lasting five years and circling the world. Darwin filled notebooks with drawings and observations of a zoo's worth of creatures from across the globe, and he collected thousands of specimens for later study.

Once home, the naturalist pondered his notes and illustrations. He saw that species collected from different locations had curiously odd characteristics compared with one another. These differences seemed key to each animal's survival in its unique environment. A revolutionary theory began to form in Darwin's mind: the theory of natural selection.

Darwin's big idea explains how all plants and animals—including humans—slowly change (or evolve) over time to improve their chances of survival. All life-forms are subject to the forces of natural selection, in which nature favors changes that help a species survive and reproduce. That in turn passes on successful adaptations to the next generation. Eventually, all these adaptations add up until one species evolves into a new one. Darwin believed that if you go back far enough in Earth's history, all life-forms evolved from a common ancestor.

Though his theory met with some controversy when he published it in his 1859 book *On the Origin of Species,* Darwin's big idea—backed by overwhelming scientific evidence and modern genetic studies—has stood the test of time.

"THERE IS GRANDEUR IN THIS VIEW OF LIFE ... FROM SO SIMPLE A BEGINNING ENDLESS FORMS MOST BEAUTIFUL AND MOST WONDERFUL HAVE BEEN, AND ARE BEING, EVOLVED." —CHARLES DARWIN

FEARLESS FACTS

→ **BORN:** February 12, 1809, Shrewsbury, England → **DIED:** April 19, 1882, Downe, England
→ **OCCUPATION:** Naturalist → **BOLDEST MOMENT:** Developing a controversial (at the time) theory for the evolution of all species

SUFFERING FOR SCIENCE
RESEARCHERS WHO RISKED IT ALL

Hazardous chemicals, contagious diseases, radioactive materials, explosive experiments—science can be a dangerous business. The geniuses who don lab coats and lead the way with their daring research sometimes risk their lives to make the next big lifesaving breakthrough. Here's to the heroes who laid everything on the line to learn.

MIRACLE WORKERS: Kent Brantly and the Ebola Doctors

On a summer morning in 2014, Dr. Kent Brantly woke up with a mild fever. Within a few days, he felt so sick that he feared his next breath might be his last. Brantly had contracted the Ebola virus, the very disease he was trying to fight while on a medical mission in the African country of Liberia. The diagnosis was like a death sentence: Tens of thousands of people have perished in West Africa from the Ebola virus, which causes patients to bleed to death.

Growing weaker by the hour, Brantly was flown back to the United States for treatment. He was offered an experimental drug called ZMapp, which cured monkeys of Ebola but had never been tested on humans. The drug saved his life. After 30 days in the hospital, he was Ebola-free. Today Dr. Brantly works in the United States to call attention to people in West Africa who have suffered from this horrible disease and to the dozens of heroic doctors working to wipe out Ebola for good.

BOLT OF INSPIRATION:
Benjamin Franklin (1706–1790)

You could come up with 50 reasons why Benjamin Franklin should be in this book, not the least of which are the U.S.A.'s 50 states, for which Franklin laid the foundation as one of the country's Founding Fathers. He helped draft and then sign the Declaration of Independence and the U.S. Constitution. An author, printer, postmaster, inventor, diplomat, and politician, Franklin was one of early America's busiest people. Today, he's considered one of the greatest Americans.

He was also a scientist. Franklin studied everything from the seafloor to the weather. In a legendary 1752 experiment, Franklin flew a

CRASH TEST GENIUS: Lawrence Patrick
(1920–2006)

When this engineering professor had a rough day at the office, he went home with the bruises to prove it. From 1960 to 1975, Patrick was the director of Wayne State University's Biomechanics Research Center in Detroit, Michigan, U.S.A. On any given workday, he might let a heavy pendulum whack him in the chest, or bang his knee over and over against a bar of solid metal, or strap himself into a speeding car that lurched to a sudden stop.

Patrick took these beatings so people in car accidents wouldn't have to. The very first automobiles didn't roll off the assembly line with seat belts, airbags, shatter-resistant windshields, and collapsible steering wheel columns. Those safety features evolved later, thanks to the work of engineers such as Patrick and his students. He needed to see the injuries people suffered in car crashes so that he could design measures to prevent them. Patrick could learn only so much by studying crash test dummies, lifelike mannequins that bend like humans but can't tell you where they hurt. To get accurate data on bruises and broken bones, Patrick's research needed a human touch. He volunteered to be that human, a real-life crash test dummy.

FO4305OZ02

GUTSY GALS

A SHINING MIND:
Marie Curie (1867–1934)

Maria "Marie" Curie became the first person in history to win two Nobel Prizes, but her breakthroughs in the study of radiation came at a terrible cost. Born Maria Sklodowska in Poland to parents who were teachers, she was fascinated by math and physics in a time when women weren't welcome in the scientific fields. She studied in secret until moving to Paris, where she met and married French physicist Pierre Curie. Suddenly, science had a power couple.

The Curies began experimenting with uranium, a mysterious metal that gives off rays similar to x-rays. Calling the phenomenon "radioactivity," Curie invented a new field of study. But as a pioneer in atomic physics, she didn't realize that radiation was dangerous. Modern scientists use lead shields and remote sensors to study radioactive materials. Curie carried radium in her pocket. In 1934, at age 66, she died of a cancer caused by her research.

kite in an electrical storm to test the properties of electricity. It wasn't the brightest move; if the lightning had struck Franklin or his kite, he would have been electrocuted. Fortunately, for the sake of the country he would help establish decades later, Franklin survived the storm with only a mild shock. He went on to invent the lightning rod, a metal object mounted on the top of a tall structure and wired to the ground. It provides a path for lightning to follow to the ground rather than passing through the building and potentially hurting the people inside.

LIFE PRESERVERS

SCIENTISTS WHO SAVED MILLIONS

KARL LANDSTEINER (1868–1943)

This Austrian biologist discovered in 1901 that people have different blood types and that only certain types are compatible with others. This discovery paved the way for safe transfusions—or transfers of blood—from healthy donors to compatible patients. Today, transfusions are the most common type of hospital procedure. Nearly 16 million blood donations are made each year, and the Red Cross estimates that just one donation can save up to three lives. Even routine surgeries would be dangerous without them.

ESTIMATED LIVES SAVED:
**MORE THAN
A BILLION**

NORMAN BORLAUG (1914–2009)

With the ultimate green thumb, this American biologist invented a tough type of wheat that grows fast even in harsh environments. His discovery might sound as bland as whole wheat toast, but it came at the right time to feed billions in danger of starving during a population explosion in the 1970s. Called the father of the green revolution, Borlaug won a pile of medals for his discovery, including the Nobel Peace Prize and the Presidential Medal of Freedom.

ESTIMATED LIVES SAVED:
**MORE THAN
A BILLION**

NUMBER OF

1 BILLION

LIVES SAVED

LOUIS PASTEUR (1822–1895)

After coming up with the theory that germs—harmful bacteria, viruses, molds, and parasites—could be transmitted from person to person, this French scientist figured out a way to kill the microscopic monsters. His technique of boiling and then cooling liquids to destroy germs became known as pasteurization. It's the reason you can chug milk with your chocolate chip cookies and not upchuck later. Pasteur also invented vaccines for anthrax and rabies, two deadly diseases.

ESTIMATED LIVES SAVED:
HUNDREDS OF MILLIONS

JONAS SALK (1914–1995)

Using himself and members of his family as test subjects, this American medical doctor discovered a vaccine for polio, a terrifying disease that killed nearly 60,000 Americans in 1952 alone. Those who don't die from polio might be paralyzed for life. Although he could've made a fortune from the vaccine, Salk refused to patent it. When asked who the patent belonged to, Salk said, "The people."

ESTIMATED LIVES SAVED:
MILLIONS

EDWARD JENNER (1749–1823)

Working in a time before scientists even knew that viruses were a thing, this English doctor discovered a way to prevent smallpox, a highly contagious disease that killed millions. He noticed that milkmaids who caught cowpox—a mild but related disease caught from milking infected cows—seemed immune to smallpox. By deliberately exposing his child patients (including his own son) to cowpox, Jenner was able to immunize them against the deadly smallpox. He is today considered the father of immunology.

ESTIMATED LIVES SAVED:
MORE THAN 500 MILLION

ALEXANDER FLEMING (1881–1955)

When this Scottish scientist returned to his lab after a summer break in 1928, he noticed he had left the lid off of one of his bacteria samples, which had grown a fuzzy coat of mold. "That's funny," he said, when he saw that the mold killed the bacteria beneath it. His accident led to the discovery of penicillin, one of the first medicines used to treat dangerous bacterial infections.

ESTIMATED LIVES SAVED:
MORE THAN 80 MILLION

JAMES HARRISON (1936–)

This Australian Good Samaritan is more of a medical marvel than a scientist. Harrison began donating blood after his own life was saved by a transfusion when he was 14. Doctors discovered that his blood contains a rare antibody capable of curing a disease that afflicts pregnant women. Harrison has been donating his special blood ever since—more than 1,100 times—enough to save more than two million babies. Known as the "man with the golden arm," he almost always donates from his right arm and says he never looks at the needle.

ESTIMATED LIVES SAVED:
MORE THAN 2 MILLION

500 MILLION

1 MILLION

STEPHEN HAWKING

THE MODERN MASTER OF THE UNIVERSE

"INTELLIGENCE IS THE ABILITY TO ADAPT TO CHANGE." —STEPHEN HAWKING

Stephen Hawking believes the sky has no limits. Blast off in a spaceship, for instance, and you'll never encounter a boundary at the edge of the universe. It's an upbeat theory for a man whose world came crashing down when he was just 21 years old. Before he earned the reputation as the most brilliant scientific mind since Einstein, Hawking was diagnosed with a serious illness. Doctors told him he would be lucky to see his 24th birthday.

MATTERS OF LIFE AND DEATH

Born exactly 300 years after the death of Galileo, Stephen Hawking seemed destined for astronomical achievements. His childhood home was part school (reading during meals was encouraged) and part amusement park (Hawking's parents raised bees and created fireworks). As a student, Hawking was bright but frequently bored. He got good grades despite short-changing studies for off-campus distractions: tinkering with electronics, inventing games, and dancing with girls.

While attending the University of Oxford in England, Hawking noticed he was getting klutzy and having a hard time speaking. His father took him to see a doctor for intense medical testing. The diagnosis: Hawking had Amyotrophic Lateral Sclerosis (ALS, aka Lou Gehrig's

FEARLESS FACTS

➔ **BORN:** January 8, 1942, Oxford, England ➔ **OCCUPATION:** Theoretical physicist
➔ **BOLDEST MOMENT:** Leading a revolution in astrophysics while overcoming physical challenges

disease). His muscles were becoming harder to control, and the condition was only going to get worse.

EXPLORING THE UNIVERSE

While such a diagnosis would send most people into a black hole of depression, Hawking threw himself into his studies of actual black holes, cosmic whirlpools that suck in everything: asteroids, planets, other stars, and even light. Building off the theories of Albert Einstein, Hawking tried to reverse engineer the workings of the universe through quantum physics—or the study of the universe at its teeniest-weeniest level.

As Hawking became famous in the world of astrophysics, his physical condition worsened. By the end of the 1960s, he relied on a wheelchair. By the 1980s, he could no longer talk. To communicate, he relied on a revolutionary computerized system to choose words by twitching the muscles of his cheek. These drawbacks didn't slow Hawking down. He had married, started a family, and achieved academic greatness. He was appointed a top professor at the University of Cambridge—a post once held by science great Sir Isaac Newton.

UP AND AWAY

Outside of the classroom, Hawking is a celebrity. He's written numerous books that simplify his complex theories for the everyday reader. He's appeared as himself in *Star Trek*, *The Big Bang Theory*, and other popular television shows. And Hawking has traveled the world, from Antarctica to the ocean floor in a submarine to the fringes of space in a plane that simulates zero gravity. Hawking turned 74 in 2016, far outliving the predictions of his doctors. Still on his to-do list: a trip to space—which makes sense for a man who believes the sky has no limits.

Hawking giving a speech called "Why We Should Go Into Space"

black hole

big bang theory

unifying theory

FROM THE HEAD OF HAWKING

➔ **FADE TO BLACK:** Black holes were once thought to munch all matter, but Hawking showed that some matter can escape in the form of radiation—now called Hawking Radiation.

➔ **BEGINNING OF THE END:** Hawking theorizes that just as the universe began in a cosmic "big bang," it will someday end up collapsing into black holes.

➔ **THEORY OF EVERYTHING:** Hawking's life's work is a "unifying theory." It combines the small picture of quantum theory with the big picture of astrophysics to explain the complete workings of the universe.

COURAGEOUS CREATORS
FIVE FEARLESS INVENTORS

When inspiration struck, these ingenious tinkerers rolled up their sleeves and devised devices and technologies that improved lives—and in some cases saved them. If you like searching the Web for microwave recipes or munching on peanut butter snacks from your seat in a passenger jet, you'll want to thank these awesome inventors ...

THOUGHT FOR FOOD: Percy Spencer (1894–1970)

The next time you zap a burrito in 60 seconds or dig into a hot bowl of microwave popcorn, spare a second to thank the American engineer whose invention has spared you hours. Percy Spencer was tinkering with a magnetron for plane-detecting radar systems in 1945 when he felt something funny in his pocket. Inside, he found that his chocolate bar had melted from exposure to microwaves—a special frequency of radio waves—emitted by the magnetron. Intrigued by the mess, Spencer grabbed some popcorn kernels and held them in front of the magnetron. Suddenly, he was responsible for two world-changing inventions at once: a new type of fast-cooking oven and microwave popcorn.

SAVIOR OF THE SOUTH:
George Washington Carver (ca 1864–1943)

Peanuts pop to mind when most people think of this brilliant botanist, who famously invented more than 300 uses—from hand lotion to gasoline—for the tasty legume. But George Washington Carver also saved thousands of poor families from starvation in the American South, where he was born a slave sometime in the mid-1860s. After the practice of slavery was abolished following the Civil War, Carver eked out an education at the few schools that would accept black students before becoming a teacher at the Tuskegee Institute. There he developed and taught poor southern farmers to grow crops other than cotton, which sapped the soil of nutrients. By planting peanuts or sweet potatoes every other year, the farmers were able to rejuvenate their fields while feeding their families more nutritious foods.

SOAR WINNERS: Orville Wright and Wilbur Wright (1871–1948) and (1867–1912)

When astronaut Neil Armstrong touched down on the moon in 1969 (read all about it on pages 70–71), he carried a scrap of the invention that made the trip possible: a bit of the wooden propeller from the Wright Flyer, the world's first powered heavier-than-air flying machine. It was built by two brothers from Ohio, U.S.A., who began experimenting with flight controls, lightweight engines, and wing designs at their bicycle shop in 1899.

Four years later, their Wright Flyer was ready for liftoff. They transported it to a beach at Kitty Hawk, North Carolina, U.S.A., where the constant sea breezes had helped them with earlier glider experiments. Only a few spectators and reporters witnessed Orville Wright take the machine on its maiden flight. It lasted just 12 seconds and covered 120 feet (36.6 m), but this achievement ushered in the era of flight and took humanity to new heights.

WEB WONDER: Timothy Berners-Lee (1955–)

No single inventor can claim credit for the Internet, which dates back to the early 1960s when computer scientists began brainstorming a system for researchers, educators, and government agencies to share information through their computers. But English computer scientist Timothy Berners-Lee helped turn the Internet into a tool for everybody. In 1989, he invented hypertext transfer protocol (HTTP), a language of rules that lets computers share information over the Internet through a system of linked pages that Berners-Lee called the World Wide Web. Berners-Lee's system blossomed into an essential worldwide resource for information, communication, and cute kitty videos.

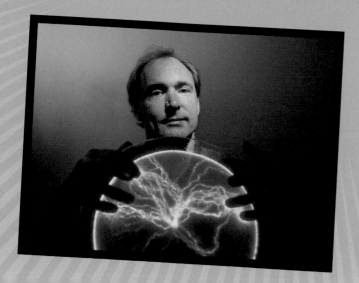

GUTSY GALS

BULLETPROOF BRAINIAC: Stephanie Kwolek (1923–2014)

As a kid, Stephanie Kwolek loved fabric and sewing. But instead of becoming a fashion designer, she became one of the world's first female research chemists. While working at the DuPont chemical company, she was assigned to develop a strong, lightweight fiber to be used in car tires. One day, she put a liquid she had created into a spinning machine, and the molecules in the liquid lined up in long chains, creating a fiber. That fiber became Kevlar: a lightweight, fireproof material five times as strong as steel. Today, Kevlar is used to make everything from kayaks to spacecraft to—most famously— bulletproof body armor. Since police officers started using Kevlar body armor in 1975, Kwolek's invention has saved about 3,000 lives.

MICHIO KAKU

LOOKING AT TOMORROW TODAY

"OUR GRANDKIDS WILL LEAD THE LIVES OF THE GODS OF MYTHOLOGY."
-MICHIO KAKU

We'll chat with friends using our minds instead of our mouths! Sensors on bathroom mirrors will detect diseases before they become dangerous! Robots will drive us to school, remove our tonsils, and devour the dust from under our beds! The future according to Dr. Michio Kaku—physicist, television host, and author—might sound too good to be true. But instead of science fiction, Kaku insists it's science fact.

Born in California, U.S.A., Kaku took an interest in physics before he was even in high school. He built a particle accelerator—a device that smashes atoms to create exotic anti-matter—in his parents' basement for a science fair project. After studying physics at Harvard University, he became a professor at the City College of New York. Kaku shares Stephen Hawking's goal of finding a unifying theory that combines quantum theory with Einstein's findings to explain the complete workings of the universe.

But while Kaku's textbooks on string field theory and other head-spinning theoretical subjects are required reading for graduate students, everyone else turns to him for his visions of the future. As a futurist, Kaku studies today's trends to predict what life will be like tomorrow. He bases his predictions on the laws of physics and surveys hundreds of scientists from all over the world for their thoughts.

Microscopic robots, he says, will someday scoot through our bloodstream and repair damaged tissue—even rebuild bad organs—extending our lives considerably. Computers will be hidden in our cars, clothes, and appliances, changing how we interact with the world, while special contact lenses will project the Internet onto everything we see. These wonders are closer than you think, Kaku insists.

FEARLESS FACTS

→ **BORN:** January 24, 1947, San Jose, California, U.S.A.   → **OCCUPATION:** Futurist, physicist
→ **BOLDEST MOMENT:** Offering predictions of a future that fill us with hope rather than dread

TAYLOR WILSON

SCIENCE'S RISING STAR

"THERE'S NOTHING THAT'S IMPOSSIBLE TO ME. YOU CAN ASK MY PARENTS."
—TAYLOR WILSON

When Taylor Wilson was 12, he wanted to build the sun in his family's garage. Two years later, he succeeded. Wilson became the youngest person to harness nuclear fusion, the process of smashing atoms under temperatures exceeding 500 million°F (260 million°C) to release vast amounts of energy—the same process that powers the sun.

Wilson's parents realized they had a science prodigy on their hands not long after he was born. Eager to feed his bottomless appetite for science, Wilson's grandmother bought him a book called *The Radioactive Boy Scout* when he was 11. It was the tale of a Michigan, U.S.A., teenager who tried to build an atomic reactor in his backyard but instead created a toxic mess that had to be cleaned up by government agents in radiation suits. Wilson believed he could do better than the boy in the story, especially with help from his parents. He threw himself into the study of nuclear physics, electrical engineering, and other complex subjects. When his grandmother became sick with cancer, Wilson wondered if he could create the expensive radioactive materials used to treat patients with the disease. He set up a laboratory in the garage to study rocks that literally glowed in the dark from radioactivity.

Wilson's parents connected him with other pioneers in the field and enrolled him in the Davidson Academy of Nevada, a school for gifted students. There he found the teachers and tools he needed to build his fusion reactor. He followed that feat with a device that could detect hidden radioactive bombs. In 2012 Wilson met with President Barack Obama to show him how the device worked.

FEARLESS FACTS

➡ **BORN:** May 7, 1994, Texarkana, Arkansas, U.S.A. ➡ **OCCUPATION:** Nuclear physicist
➡ **BOLDEST MOMENT:** Building a nuclear fusion reactor

MOMENT OF BRAVERY

Study participants were asked to do something shocking. Did they comply or resist?

THE SITUATION

In the summer of 1961, an advertisement appeared in newspapers around New Haven, Connecticut, U.S.A., seeking men to take part in a "scientific study of memory and learning" at Yale University. Volunteers who answered the ad were met at the school by an experimenter in a white lab coat who introduced them to a mild-mannered fellow volunteer. The experimenter then asked both volunteers to each take a crumpled piece of paper from his hand. One had the word "teacher" printed on it. The other volunteer's paper read "learner." These roles set the stage for one of the most famous experiments in the history of psychology.

The volunteer "teacher" was given a seat at a desk topped with a control panel marked with the words "Shock Generator." It was lined with a bank of switches of increasing electrical voltages labeled from "Slight Shock" to "Danger: Severe Shock." The final switch was marked only with "XXX." Meanwhile, the volunteer playing the "learner" stepped out of view into an adjacent room, where he was connected to electrodes attached to the shocking machine.

It was the teacher's job to ask the learner a series of simple word puzzles. Each time the learner gave an incorrect response, the experimenter in the white lab coat ordered the teacher to flip a switch on the control panel to zap the learner—and these shocks grew in severity with each mistake the learner made. The first few jolts caused merely a mild tingle. But soon, after giving several wrong answers, the learner began to howl in agony. The teacher looked to the experimenter for some direction. "Please continue," said the man in the white coat.

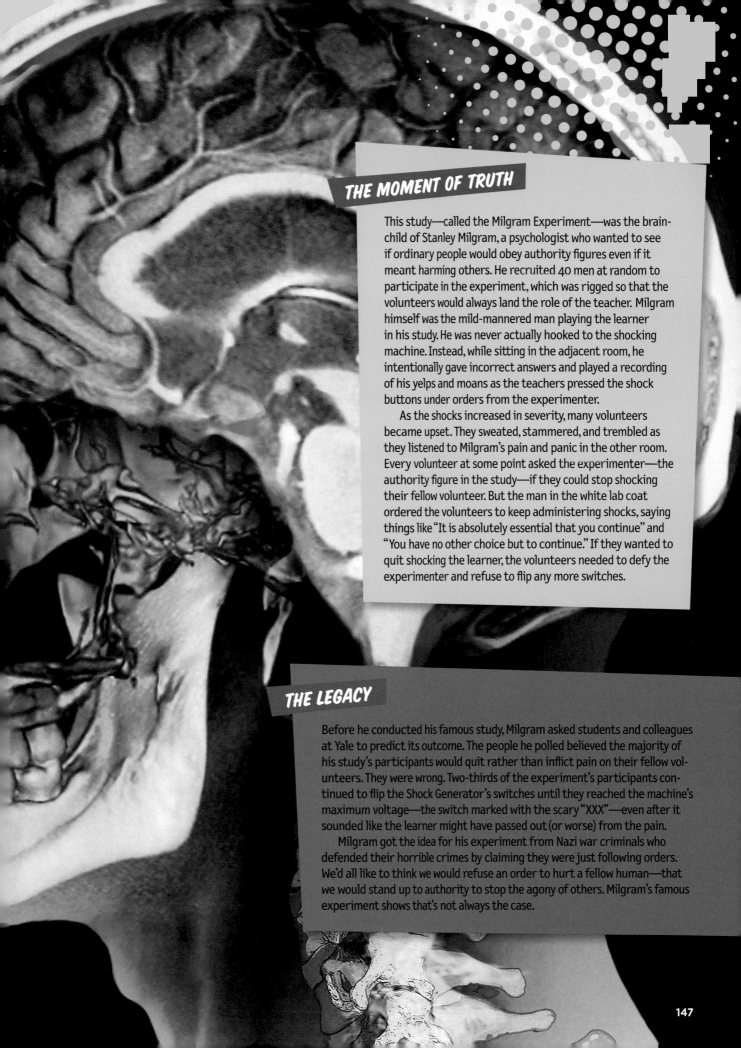

THE MOMENT OF TRUTH

This study—called the Milgram Experiment—was the brain-child of Stanley Milgram, a psychologist who wanted to see if ordinary people would obey authority figures even if it meant harming others. He recruited 40 men at random to participate in the experiment, which was rigged so that the volunteers would always land the role of the teacher. Milgram himself was the mild-mannered man playing the learner in his study. He was never actually hooked to the shocking machine. Instead, while sitting in the adjacent room, he intentionally gave incorrect answers and played a recording of his yelps and moans as the teachers pressed the shock buttons under orders from the experimenter.

As the shocks increased in severity, many volunteers became upset. They sweated, stammered, and trembled as they listened to Milgram's pain and panic in the other room. Every volunteer at some point asked the experimenter—the authority figure in the study—if they could stop shocking their fellow volunteer. But the man in the white lab coat ordered the volunteers to keep administering shocks, saying things like "It is absolutely essential that you continue" and "You have no other choice but to continue." If they wanted to quit shocking the learner, the volunteers needed to defy the experimenter and refuse to flip any more switches.

THE LEGACY

Before he conducted his famous study, Milgram asked students and colleagues at Yale to predict its outcome. The people he polled believed the majority of his study's participants would quit rather than inflict pain on their fellow volunteers. They were wrong. Two-thirds of the experiment's participants continued to flip the Shock Generator's switches until they reached the machine's maximum voltage—the switch marked with the scary "XXX"—even after it sounded like the learner might have passed out (or worse) from the pain.

Milgram got the idea for his experiment from Nazi war criminals who defended their horrible crimes by claiming they were just following orders. We'd all like to think we would refuse an order to hurt a fellow human—that we would stand up to authority to stop the agony of others. Milgram's famous experiment shows that's not always the case.

OUTSTANDING ANIMALS

Spot might not seem particularly courageous when he chews your shoes, and Mrs. Whiskers is hardly a role model when she spits a dead mouse onto your sofa. But, believe it or not, inside your beloved pet beats the heart of a hero. Prepare to paw through pages showcasing the selfless side of wildlife, from daredevil dolphins to pigeons that helped win a war.

A military dog accompanies U.S. Army soldiers on a mission in Kandahar, Afghanistan.

SERGEANT STUBBY

MAN'S BRAVEST FRIEND

Before he helped capture an enemy spy, before he was invited to the White House, and before he became the most famous and decorated combat dog of World War I, the Boston terrier mutt named Stubby was just a stray that stowed away on a troop ship. He'd been hidden in the ship's coal bin by J. Robert Conroy, an Army private who had found the dog—and named him for his nub of a tail—wandering the training camp on the fields of Yale University, in Connecticut, U.S.A., in 1917. Conroy sneaked the lovable little dog all the way to France, hiding him under his coat to get him off the ship.

But Stubby's adventure seemed nearly over before it began when Conroy's commanding officer discovered he had been hiding the dog. (Animals were forbidden at the French base.) What Stubby did next became a military legend: He saluted with a paw against his eye, a trick he had learned from Conroy. Instead of kicking Stubby out of the camp, Conroy's commanding officer made him the official mascot of the infantry regiment. The soldiers loved Stubby, a source of happiness during a grim time. He learned their drills and bugle calls. In February 1918, he went to war.

FEARLESS FACTS

→ **BORN:** 1917, New Haven, Connecticut, U.S.A. → **DIED:** 1926, Washington, D.C., U.S.A.
→ **OCCUPATION:** Mascot of a U.S. Army infantry division in World War I
→ **BOLDEST MOMENT:** Capturing an enemy snoop

FURRY FIGHTER

Stubby was only supposed to be the mascot, but he served alongside his fellow soldiers on the front lines in France. He used his supersensitive nose to detect poison gas, barking an alarm when he got a whiff of the deadly fumes. He would listen for injured or missing soldiers and find them on the battlefield, yipping until help arrived. With his superior hearing, Stubby could detect the faint whistle of enemy shells and bark a warning to his comrades. When Stubby encountered a German spy snooping on the battlefield, he chomped his leg and slowed him down until American soldiers could capture him. For his bravery, Stubby was given an honorary promotion to sergeant.

DECORATED DOG

He fought in 17 battles. When Stubby was injured in a grenade attack, his comrades rushed him to the hospital for surgery. He recovered and returned to the trenches until injuries forced him to retire from battle. Even then he served his country, visiting wounded soldiers and boosting morale. After the war, Stubby appeared in parades and visited with three presidents at the White House. He wasn't the first war dog—tales of courageous canines in battle go back to ancient Greece—but Sergeant Stubby was one of the most famous, an example for all pooch troops to come.

Sergeant Stubby in France in 1919 (above left) and on a float in a Washington, D.C., parade in 1921 (above right)

COMBAT CANINES

Your pooch might know how to roll over and shake hands, but can he parachute into enemy territory? Highly trained military working dogs have been skydiving behind enemy lines since World War II. Typically of the stocky Belgian shepherd Malinois breed, today's tough pups wear bulletproof armor equipped with cameras so they can scout ahead or send pictures from hard-to-reach places. They even wear protective goggles—called doggles.

Canines must train and practice their skills to become military working dogs (above and right).

WHO'S A GOOD DOG?
FIVE HEROIC HOUNDS

Smart, playful, affectionate, scrappy, loyal—the list of your pooch's positive qualities goes on and on. But is Fido fearless as well as friendly? Does he have what it takes to save the day? Shake paws with five daring dogs that rose to the occasion instead of rolling over ...

THE POLICE DOG: Trakr (1994–2009)

Dogs have a superpower—a sense of smell that's thousands of times more sensitive than yours—and Trakr the German shepherd used his power for good. He joined more than 300 other search-and-rescue dogs trained to sniff out survivors after the World Trade Center collapsed on September 11, 2001. Bounding through the rubble with his handler, Trakr pinpointed the last survivor of the attack. Genelle Guzman-McMillan had been buried beneath tons of concrete and steel for 27 hours. Trakr passed away in 2009, but he was such an extraordinary dog that scientists at a South Korean lab cloned him five times.

THE ST. BERNARD: Barry (1800–1814)

Bred for their thick fur, excellent sense of direction, and broad chests that smash a path through deep powder, St. Bernards are famous for having saved the lives of about 2,000 people lost in the snowy Swiss Alps. For nearly 200 years, starting in the early 18th century, monks living in the stormy St. Bernard's Pass between Italy and Switzerland dispatched these dogs in packs to sniff out lost travelers and either lead them to the monastery or lay on them for warmth until help arrived. The most famous of the pack was Barry, who saved more than 40 people, including a boy he found sleeping in a crevice. Barry licked the boy to wake him up, then carried him back to the safety and warmth of the monastery.

THE SLED DOG: Togo (1913–1929)

When a deadly disease broke out in the remote Alaskan village of Nome in 1925, the residents didn't have many options. Out of range of planes and ships, they relied on their trusty sled dogs. Teams of heroic huskies worked in relays to retrieve a lifesaving serum, but a dog named Togo outran them all. In just three days, Togo and his team pulled a sled loaded with medicine nearly 200 miles (322 km) across treacherous ice floes and through blizzards that blinded his human driver. He saved the town but remained an unsung hound: A husky named Balto, who ran the last leg of the trip, got most of the credit.

THE EXPLOSIVE-DETECTION DOG: Carlos

THE ASTROMUTT: Laika (ca 1954–1957)

GUTSY GALS

This dashing yellow Labrador was a soldier's best friend. First in Iraq and then in Afghanistan, Carlos served nearly five continuous years in the military, searching buildings, roads, and other places for hidden explosives. His superior sniffing skills saved the lives of many American soldiers. When he started developing arthritis and eye problems in 2011, Carlos retired from the service and returned to

the United States, where he was adopted by a loving family. But his mission wasn't over yet. Carlos became an ambassador for all military working dogs, visiting clubs, schools, and even Washington, D.C., as a war dog representative for a congressional briefing. In 2013, the American Humane Association named Carlos its Military Hero Dog of the Year.

Before the first manned space flights in the 1950s, scientists weren't sure if humans could survive a rocket ride into Earth's orbit, where astronauts would experience weightlessness and higher levels of radiation. So they sent test flights crewed by a small zoo's worth of animals: fruit flies, monkeys, mice, and dogs. The first pooch to orbit our planet was a terrier mutt named Laika, just two years old and plucked from the streets of Moscow barely more than a week before her historic launch. Her 1957 mission paved the way for the first manned spaceflight by Russian cosmonaut Yuri Gagarin four years later.

CHER AMI THE PIGEON

THE BIRD THAT CARRIED THE WORD

Trapped in a dense French forest behind enemy lines, the American soldiers of the 77th division were facing annihilation in the fall of 1918. U.S. Army artillerymen were mistakenly shelling the 77th's position even as enemy troops closed in. The division's commander desperately needed to send headquarters a message: Stop the shelling and send help! Instead of reaching for a radio or a phone, he attached a message to a small bird with green and purple plumage. The pigeon launched into the sky and was immediately dispatched by enemy fire. A second bird met the same fate. Only one pigeon remained, a brave little bird named Cher Ami. The commander attached a message to the pigeon's leg and sent the bird skyward.

During World War I, before the invention of small field radios, the U.S. Army Signal Corps in France relied on 600 specially trained carrier pigeons to ferry messages between headquarters and soldiers in the field. Cher Ami, which means "dear friend" in French, was one such bird. Enemy fire filled the air as soon as Cher Ami cleared the American camp. One bullet pierced his chest. Another hit the leg that carried the 77th's vital message. Despite these injuries, Cher Ami carried the message 25 miles (40 km) in just over an hour to division headquarters, completing his mission and saving nearly 200 lives. Army medics attended to Cher Ami's wounds and outfitted the bird with a wooden leg. It wasn't until the patriot pigeon died that scientists discovered a twist ending in this tale: Cher Ami wasn't a male, as everyone had thought. The brave bird had been a girl.

> COMMUNICATION IS CRUCIAL IN ANY BATTLE; CONFUSION CAN REIGN WITHOUT IT.

GUTSY GALS

FEARLESS FACTS

→ **BORN:** Great Britain → **DIED:** June 13, 1919, New Jersey, U.S.A.
→ **OCCUPATION:** Homing pigeon → **BOLDEST MOMENT:** Saving a "Lost Battalion" of American soldiers during World War I

WILLIE
THE PARROT

THE WORLD'S BEST BIRD BABYSITTER

Mama, baby! Mama, baby!" Willie the parrot shouted an alarm and flapped his wings. He was trying to get the attention of his owner, Morgan Howard, who had just stepped out of the kitchen to use the bathroom. The Colorado, U.S.A., babysitter heard Willie's panicked shouts and knew something must be amiss; Willie was normally a quiet bird. When she rushed back into the room, Howard found the toddler she was babysitting at the kitchen table and turning blue. The child was choking!

Howard rushed into action. She gave the two-year-old the Heimlich maneuver to dislodge the food that was causing the choking. When the child began breathing again, Willie immediately calmed down. Howard's quick thinking saved the day, but without Willie's warning, she might not have gotten to the toddler in time. In 2009, the Denver chapter of the Red Cross gave Willie its annual Animal Lifesaver Award, which in previous years had been awarded exclusively to dogs. The shy little parrot remained silent for the entire ceremony.

Parrots are hardly bird-brained. Not only can they copy human speech, but researchers have also found that some parrots actually understand what they're saying when they squawk in English.

WILLIE SHOUTED AND FLAPPED HIS WINGS TO GET THE ATTENTION OF HIS OWNER.

FEARLESS FACTS

➔ **OCCUPATION:** Pet   ➔ **BOLDEST MOMENT:** Helping save the life of a choking baby

LENDING A PAW
ANIMALS HELPING ANIMALS

Sure, animals are *our* superpals, but we're hardly the only species they play nice with. Animals also develop some pretty amazing relationships with each other. And in the dangerous dog-eat-dog world of wildlife, unusual alliances can even be crucial to survival. These courageous creatures swooped in for the save when fellow feathered, furry, or finned friends were in need.

HELPFUL, HELPFUL HIPPO

The crocodile picked on the wrong prey when it sunk its teeth into a young wildebeest trying to cross a river in Kenya's Masai Mara Reserve in 2011. Just as the croc was about to drag the bleating beast underwater to its doom—splash!—a heroic hippopotamus charged to the rescue.

Although they look klutzy and cute, hippos are powerful and territorial animals that tend to attack anything—including people—without warning. (Some people in Africa believe the hippo kills more humans than any other large animal.) In this case, the hippo frightened off the croc, then nudged the shaken wildebeest to shore. People on safari have also witnessed hippos saving zebras, impalas, and other animals, leading experts to wonder if these ill-tempered creatures have a sweet side.

KILLER THE RHINO RANGER

You wouldn't think a thick-skinned, two-ton (1.8-t) beast armed with a three-foot (1-m) horn would need help from a 65-pound (29-kg) dog. But in Africa, where greedy hunters hunt rhinoceroses illegally for their price-less ivory horns, a new breed of highly trained dogs are joining the fight against poaching (the illegal hunting of rhinoceroses, elephants, and other threatened animals). Killer the Belgian Malinois is one of these courageous canines.

Strapped into a helicopter with his team of armed rangers, Killer soars over South Africa's Kruger National Park on the hunt for rhino poachers. He can track their scent for miles in the thick savanna brush and detect the smell of ivory smuggled in cars and suitcases. Even when poachers drop

REX TO THE RESCUE!

Rex, a German shorthaired pointer, was off for a walk with his owner on Australia's southern coast in 2008 when they came across a heartbreaking sight: a kangaroo that had been killed by a car. But Rex's superior senses picked up on something his owner did not. Dogs live in a three-dimensional world of odors, which can transmit all sorts of information that humans can't detect. It took just a few sniffs of the dead kangaroo to tell Rex all he needed to know. He returned to the spot later in the day and gently pulled a squirming baby kangaroo from its mother's pouch.

Rex carried the baby back home, and the tiny kangaroo was sent to a wildlife sanctuary to make a full recovery—but not before he snuggled and licked his rescuer. Naturally, the cute photos of Rex and his friend went viral on the Internet.

AUNTIE OTTER JOY

GUTSY GALS

Five-day-old sea otter Joy was found stranded on Twin Lakes Beach in Santa Cruz, California, U.S.A., in August 1998. Rescuers patiently taught her to forage for food and released her into the wild in December 1998. But the friendly otter developed a habit of coming up to kayakers and divers, which wasn't safe for the people or the otter. So staff at the Monterey Bay Aquarium—which through its Sea Otter Program raises and releases stranded pups and finds homes for otters that can't return to the wild—took her in as a permanent resident. There, Joy became a substitute mother to abandoned otter babies and helped raise 16 pups, more than any other surrogate in the aquarium's history. That earned her the nickname Super Mom—and the love of everyone who visited the aquarium.

stinky chili peppers on their trail to try to cover their scent, Killer's nose knows the difference. In 2015, he led his handlers to arrest at least 15 poachers. He was such a success that Kruger rangers plan to increase their number of tracking dogs to more than 40. In other parts of Africa, trained dogs like Killer are used to hunt and capture poachers who kill elephants for their ivory.

Though rhino populations have increased in recent years thanks to conservation efforts and antipoaching measures, the demand for rhino horns continues—especially for use in traditional Asian medicine, where it is made into a powder and thought to be able to cure a variety of illnesses.

HEEL, SIT, HEAL!

HOUNDS TRAINED TO HELP

Pooches and people go way back—as far back as 30,000 years ago, when humans began tossing morsels to wolves in return for protection and help with hunting. They evolved into our best friends, becoming attuned to our feelings and needs, which is why canines are easy—and eager—to train for a variety of careers. We may think these assistance dogs are heroes, but they're just happy to do their jobs.

THERAPY DOGS

This canine career started with Smoky, a tiny Yorkshire terrier found in a foxhole by an American soldier during World War II. Doctors noticed something miraculous when Smoky showed his furry face at a military hospital. The spirits of the wounded soldiers rose whenever Smoky wandered by. Today, therapy dogs are chosen for their genial nature, good behavior, and snuggling abilities, spreading cheer to people in hospitals, retirement homes, and areas struck by disaster.

SERVICE DOGS

Seeing Eye dogs—canines trained to guide the blind—leap to mind when you think of service dogs, but they're not the only kind of assisting canine. So-called hearing dogs are trained to nudge their hearing-impaired owners when they notice particular sounds (doorbells, telephones, smoke alarms, and more) and then lead their owners to the source of the sound. Mobility dogs help physically challenged owners up from their chairs or offer extra balance for people who need it. Such caring canines are nothing new; references to guide dogs date back nearly 400 years!

MEDICAL DOGS

These healing hero hounds come in two varieties. The first group, medical-response dogs, are trained to recognize the signs of oncoming attacks, such as epileptic seizures, asthma attacks, and low blood sugar in people with diabetes. The dogs bark in a special way to warn their owner of an oncoming episode—and some even dig out medication or bring the telephone.

Medical-detection dogs, meanwhile, go one step beyond and use their superior sense of smell to actually detect types of cancer before they become life-threatening. The diagnosing abilities of these dogs is still being studied, but such dogs have proven more reliable than lab tests at sniffing out skin cancers and tumors.

MAN'S OTHER BEST FRIENDS

Cats, horses, hamsters, birds, and even llamas have all taken on therapy duty ...

Pisco the llama visits elderly and ill patients to give them a dose of furry friendship. Who wouldn't want a hug from one of these humpless camels?

Pisco

Magic the miniature therapy horse was named Most Heroic Pet in America in 2010 by the American Association of Retired Persons after she broke the silent spell of a patient who hadn't spoken in years. "Isn't she beautiful?" the patient said when she laid eyes on the sweet little horse.

Magic

Doves lift the spirits of patients under the care of hospice, organizations that look after the terminally ill.

THE DOLPHINS OF MONTEREY

LENDING A FIN TO THEIR FELLOW MAMMAL

Surfer Todd Endris was 50 yards (46 m) from shore on a summer morning in 2007, watching a buddy catch a wave nearby, when something big hit him from below and knocked him into the air. That's when he saw the great white shark returning for a second attack. It sank its titanic teeth into Endris's torso and dragged him underwater. He lashed out with his feet and arms until the shark released him, only to bite him a third time. Now bleeding heavily from several wounds, Endris wouldn't survive a fourth attack.

He began paddling weakly toward shore as the water turned red around him. His friends were too far away to help him. But luckily for Endris, he had other allies nearby.

FINNED FOES

Shark attacks are incredibly rare. More people perish from mishaps taking selfies than in the jaws of a hungry shark. And for every person who dies in the jaws of Jaws, about two million sharks die at the hands of humans. But attacks do happen, and surfers are at a higher risk of being bitten. Seen from below, a surfer is a dead ringer for a sea lion: a favorite snack of the great white shark.

Endris was surfing in Monterey, California, U.S.A., within the so-called Red Triangle breeding ground for these fearsome fish. The shark that attacked him was about

> TALES OF DOLPHINS DARTING TO THE RESCUE OF SAILORS IN TROUBLE GO BACK TO ANCIENT GREECE.

FEARLESS FACTS

→ **COMMON NAME:** Bottlenose dolphins → **HABITAT:** Warm waters around the world
→ **AVERAGE SIZE:** 10 to 14 feet (3–4.3 m) → **AVERAGE LIFE SPAN:** 45 to 50 years in the wild
→ **BOLDEST MOMENT:** Shielding a surfer from a great white shark

12 feet (3.7 m) long, big enough to fit the tall surfer into its mouth. As Endris paddled toward shore, dreading the next attack, the water exploded around him. A school of bottle-nose dolphins had come to his rescue! They began leaping over and swimming beneath him, forming a wall between human and shark.

FINNED FRIENDS

More than 30 species of dolphins—including orcas (aka killer whales) and the Atlantic bottlenose dolphin made famous on TV and in aquarium shows—roam the world's oceans and rivers. Intensely social animals, they team up in groups called pods to look after each other and accomplish tasks, such as herding fish for food and protecting younger dolphins from sharks. They also have a history of helping humans. Tales of dolphins darting to the rescue of sailors in trouble go back to ancient Greece.

Whether Endris's new dolphin friends kept the shark at bay or just scared it away, no one knows. But the great white never returned for a fourth bite. Endris's brave human buddies paddled out to help him ashore, while his new marine mammal pals kept circling and protecting the wounded surfer. When they got him on the beach, Endris's friends bound his leg with a surf leash to stop the bleeding and called for an ambulance. He had lost half his blood in the attack and required more than 500 stitches, but Endris recovered and in time returned to surfing. The dolphins didn't stick around to accept any awards or pose for photos, but Endris will never forget the day they saved his life.

Surfer Todd Endris (left) and his surfboard damaged by the shark attack (below)

DOLPHINS TO THE RESCUE

➲ 2000, GULF OF MANFREDONIA, ITALY: A dolphin the locals called Filippo pushed a 14-year-old boy to safety after he fell from his father's boat and nearly drowned.

➲ 2004, RED SEA, EGYPT: Dolphins led a rescue team in the direction of 12 divers adrift after they were swept away from their dive boat.

➲ 2011, FLORIDA, U.S.A.: Dolphins making a commotion in a canal alerted a woman nearby to the presence of a lost dog in the water.

➲ 2014, COOK STRAIT, NEW ZEALAND: A pod of 10 dolphins swarmed a British long-distance swimmer, shielding him from a shark, as he completed a fund-raising marathon for whales and dolphin conservation.

A DIFFERENT BREED
UNLIKELY HELPERS

Dogs and dolphins get all the glory for charging to the rescue, but they're not the only animals capable of saving the day. From land mine–finding rats to a bear that helped win a war, these creatures walk on the wilder side of wildlife assistance ...

LOOKING FOR TROUBLE:
Mine-Sniffing Rats

If the thought of a scurrying rat makes you retch, then maybe the "demining" rats of Cambodia will make you rave for these rodents. A Belgian mine-clearing company called Apopo has been training rats to sniff out land mines and other explosives for the past 15 years, ever since they discovered that African giant pouched rats have bad eyesight but an excellent sense of smell. These specially trained rodents can find explosives better than high-tech detecting equipment. The rats are saving lives in Cambodia, where millions of land mines and other explosives lie hidden in the countryside, deadly leftovers from decades of conflict. Rats that find mines scratch at the ground, signaling their human handlers to diffuse the device before someone accidentally steps on it.

SAVING HIS OWNER'S BACON: Lucky the Pig

Oink! Oink! Squeal! Waking up to the screams of a panicked pig might sound like a nightmare. But for Ina Farler and her two grandchildren, the rude awakening saved their lives! In 2014 their pet pig, Lucky, began squealing and leaping on the bedroom furniture before dawn at their home in Illinois, U.S.A. When Farler turned on the lights to see what was wrong, she saw smoke. The home was on fire! She gathered up her grandchildren and ran to safety with Lucky following behind. It's well known that pigs are smart pets: Researchers have taught them how to play video games and even to take a shower when they're hot. Who knew they were also heroes?

GENTLE GIANT:
Jambo the Gorilla

When five-year-old Levan Merritt tumbled into the gorilla enclosure of the Durrell Wildlife Park on the European island of Jersey in 1986, a towering silverback gorilla named Jambo approached the boy's unconscious form. Spectators feared the worst was about to happen. But instead of attacking Merritt, Jambo stood over him, protecting the boy from the other gorillas in the enclosure. He even nudged Merritt and rubbed his back until the boy woke up and began to cry. Jambo also led the other gorillas away so zoo workers could rescue the boy. Jambo's good deed gained the ape worldwide fame.

BEARING ARMS: Wojtek the Bear

Donated as a cub to the Polish Army, this six-foot (1.8-m)-tall Syrian brown bear was more than just a mascot for the military during World War II. To skirt a rule that animals were not allowed to accompany soldiers into combat, Wojtek was officially enlisted into an artillery supply company. Now a soldier, "Private" Wojtek could follow the troops to battle in Italy, where his immense strength came in handy. Wojtek tirelessly carried crates of shells for Allied gun crews during an intense battle to liberate Rome, which earned him a promotion to corporal. After the war, Corporal Wojtek was immortalized in several statues, and bears were added to the list of species—including dogs, horses, pigeons, and even dolphins—that serve in war.

HOPPING TO THE RESCUE:
Dory the Rabbit

GUTSY GALS

One day in January 2004, Simon Steggall of Cambridgeshire, England, came home from a long day at work and sat down in his favorite chair, looking forward to relaxing in front of the TV. Instead, he slipped into a diabetic coma—a potentially deadly complication from diabetes. He could still feel and hear, but he couldn't speak or move: He was trapped in his own body. Steggall's wife just thought he was napping, but their pet, Dory, a 21-pound (10-kg) Flemish giant rabbit, knew better. Dory, who wasn't allowed on the furniture, broke the rules and jumped on Steggall, thumping on his chest and licking his face. It was then that Steggall's wife knew something was wrong. She called the paramedics, who were able to save Steggall's life—thanks to the brave bunny.

163

SIMON
THE UNSINKABLE

HE KEPT THE CREW AFLOAT

SIMON POUNCED DAILY ON THE RATS RAIDING THE SHIP'S DWINDLING SUPPLIES.

The British warship *Amethyst* was steaming up the Yangtze River in 1949 when it came under attack from Chinese gun batteries on shore. Among the wounded was Simon, a black-and-white cat rescued from the dockyards of Hong Kong the year before and taken aboard as the ship's official cat.

Going back to ancient times, sailors have welcomed cats aboard their ships as members of the crew. Cats chase rats, and rats are bad for boats, chewing through ropes, sails, and wiring. Even worse, they can devour crucial supplies of food. A ship's cat keeps the rats under control while crew members get a morale boost from their purring mascot.

When *Amethyst* medical personnel found Simon bleeding on the deck, they patched him up but feared he wouldn't survive the night. Meanwhile, the ship was stuck on the riverbank and under constant threat of the Chinese artillery. For the next three months, the *Amethyst* was stranded without food or supplies while the British government negotiated for its rescue. When rats hidden deep in the hull began raiding the ship's dwindling stores, Simon was ready. He had recovered from his injuries and began pouncing on at least one rat each day.

Thanks to Simon's rat snatching, the ship's supplies lasted long enough for its crew to refloat the boat and make a daring escape to sea. He was hailed as a hero in England and awarded a special medal given only to animals at war. When poor Simon died from a virus while under quarantine, he was buried with full military honors.

FEARLESS FACTS

➔ **BORN:** 1947, Hong Kong ➔ **DIED:** November 28, 1949, Surrey, England ➔ **OCCUPATION:** Ship's cat
➔ **BOLDEST MOMENT:** Protecting a stranded warship's dwindling food supplies from a rat infestation

ETHIOPIA'S HERO LIONS

ON THE PROWL FOR BAD GUYS

Police and relatives scrambled in 2005 to find a 12-year-old girl who'd been kidnapped from her Ethiopian village. A week later, they found her safe but with an alarming trio of companions—lions! The big cats had frightened away the girl's abductors and stood guard over her until police arrived. When the police came, the lions walked calmly back into the forest. It was as if they knew they had completed their mission.

Of the four big cat species (lions, tigers, jaguars, and leopards), lions are the champions of chomp. Their awesome jaws are more powerful than a grizzly bear's! Although lions are known for their courage and intense social bonds—they're the only big cats that live in groups, called prides—they also have a reputation for attacking humans on rare occasions. (Only Bengal tigers are more dangerous, responsible for killing more humans than the other three species.)

A wildlife expert believes this particular trio of lions rescued the girl because her plight appealed to their social instincts. Perhaps the lions mistook her cries of fear for a lion cub in danger. Whatever the reason, the girl had a tale to tell when she was reunited with her family. Police, meanwhile, managed to track down and arrest four of her kidnappers, who no doubt had their own tale to tell.

THE BIG CATS HAD FRIGHTENED AWAY THE GIRL'S ABDUCTORS, THEN STOOD GUARD OVER HER.

FEARLESS FACTS

➔ **COMMON NAME:** African lion ➔ **HABITAT:** Savanna grasslands of Africa ➔ **AVERAGE SIZE:** 4.5 to 6.5 feet (1.4–2 m) for their head and body ➔ **AVERAGE LIFE SPAN:** 10 to 14 years in the wild ➔ **BOLDEST MOMENT:** Rescuing a kidnapped victim from her captors

MOMENT OF BRAVERY

This hero dog needed help. But how would he get his desperate message to rescuers?

THE SITUATION

The abandoned dog had given animal rescuers the slip for weeks. They were on a mission to track down the dog—a black Labrador mix with white patches on his chest—in a public park in Dallas, Texas, U.S.A., and take him to a foster home. But every time they got close to the clever pooch, he darted away into the thick woods too quickly for them to follow.

On a winter night in 2015, animal rescuer Marina Tarashevska was in the park trying to find the elusive pooch. Suddenly, paydirt! *Ruff! Ruff! Ruff!* The familiar dog appeared from the darkness and began barking at her. As she stepped forward, the dog inched backward, barking the entire time. And yet he wasn't running away. It's almost as if the dog wanted Tarashevska to follow him.

THE MOMENT OF TRUTH

The black dog's barking had a sense of urgency. It almost seemed like an episode of *Lassie*, that old TV show with the collie that always led the way to a daring rescue. Tarashevska was in the park with dog behaviorist John Miller, who could tell from the dog's barking and movements that he wanted the two humans to follow him. So they chose to pursue rather than try to grab him.

And it's a good thing they did. The dog led the rescuers through thick woods to a creek, where they began hearing faint yelps and mewing sounds. Casting around their flashlight, they saw something squirming in the hollow of a tree: puppies! A litter of ten was shivering beneath their mother. The puppies were in bad shape. One was nearly frozen to death.

The rescuers gathered up the puppies and their mother and took them to a loving foster home. This time, the black dog came with them.

THE LEGACY

All ten of the puppies made a fast recovery from their harrowing time out in the cold. They were taken to a foster home with their mother, who was named Mona. The black dog that had helped rescue the puppies soon joined them at the foster home, but not before getting nationwide attention on websites and news shows. The dog with no name was given a fitting new one: Hero.

AFTERWORD

YOUR TURN TO BE THE GOOD GUY!

Your tour of this hall of heroes has come to an end, but that doesn't mean your journey is complete. This book is by no means a comprehensive account of history's most courageous people—and more heroes are being made every day! According to a 2011 study, one in five Americans has done something super-duper, such as helping during an emergency, standing up to an injustice, or relinquishing something dear for a complete stranger. That's a lot of everyday heroes!

Most of the heroes in the world are ordinary people who did extraordinary things in extreme situations. You could be the next to join their ranks. The process doesn't always happen overnight—no superpower-granting bites from radioactive spiders, unfortunately—but you can do things every day to make yourself ready for your heroic moment. Here to help is Matt Langdon, author of *The Hero Field Guides* and founder of the Hero Construction Company, an organization that teaches kids and adults how to unleash their inner hero. By following his tips every day, you'll officially become a hero-in-training ...

DAILY DEEDS FOR DARING DUDES

1) FIND MORE HEROES

Heroes have their own heroes. Martin Luther King, Jr.'s hero was Mohandas Gandhi. Same with Nelson Mandela. One of the great things about this book is that you now have dozens of heroes to choose from. And when you have heroes, you'll strive to act like them. If you find yourself in an emergency situation, for instance, you could imagine what Luke

168

Skywalker would do. If you're struggling against injustice, you could ask yourself
what Václav Havel or Chiune Sugihara would do.
When you're unsure, ask yourself, *What would
my heroes do in this situation?*

2) DEVELOP A HEROIC HABIT

Practice makes perfect. To get you ready to do big good
things, you should do regular little good things. It's not
heroic to pay someone a compliment, but if you do it every
day, you will be getting used to doing nice things for others.

3) STAND OUT

It's difficult to stand up and be a hero when the situation
arises. People prefer to stay safe in the crowd; we don't like
to stick out. The best way to overcome that instinct is to
get comfortable with being uncomfortable. Maybe you
could wear a funny hat. Perhaps you could mismatch your
clothes or talk in a different voice. People will notice you—
they'll probably point at you and talk about you. They might
even laugh! If you do things a little different once a week,
you will be more ready to stand out and stand up when the
hero call comes.

4) IMAGINE

As you read the stories in this book about men who risked
it all for the good of others, did you find yourself wondering, *What would I have done in his shoes?* Look for these
moments each time you see a hero story, whether it's on
the news, in a book, or on the screen. Imagining how you
might react in a tough situation sets you up for daring
deeds should the need arise. When the time comes, you'll
know the right move.

CAN'T GET ENOUGH
HEROIC HAPPENINGS AND
TRIUMPHANT TALES?

CHECK OUT
THE BOOK OF HEROINES
FOR STORIES OF
HISTORY'S GUTSIEST GALS!

INDEX

INDEX

INDEX

FOR MY WIFE, RAMAH, WHO MAKES ALL THE HARD THINGS LOOK EASY. —C.B.

The publisher would like to thank the following people for making this book possible:
Becky Baines, Michaela Weglinski, Amanda Larsen, Lori Epstein, Christina Ascani, Grace Hill,
Alix Inchausti, Darrick McRae, Lewis Bassford, and especially Jennifer Agresta,
who worked tirelessly from start to finish.

Since 1888, the National Geographic Society has funded more than 12,000 research,
exploration, and preservation projects around the world. The Society receives funds from
National Geographic Partners LLC, funded in part by your purchase. A portion of the proceeds
from this book supports this vital work. To learn more, visit www.natgeo.com/info.

NATIONAL GEOGRAPHIC and Yellow Border Design are trademarks of
the National Geographic Society, used under license.

For more information, visit nationalgeographic.com,
call 1-800-647-5463, or write to the following address:
National Geographic Partners
1145 17th Street N.W.
Washington, D.C. 20036-4688 U.S.A.

Visit us online at nationalgeographic.com/books

For librarians and teachers: ngchildrensbooks.org

More for kids from National Geographic: kids.nationalgeographic.com

For information about special discounts for bulk purchases,
please contact National Geographic Books Special Sales: ngspecsales@ngs.org

For rights or permissions inquiries,
please contact National Geographic Books Subsidiary Rights: ngbookrights@ngs.org

Designed by Amanda Larsen

Hardcover ISBN: 978-1-4263-2553-3
Reinforced library binding ISBN: 978-1-4263-2554-0

Printed in Hong Kong
16/THK/1